AF610566

Divine Intent

Understanding God's True Purpose in Creating a World of Grandeur and Beauty

Paul J. Taylor

DIVINE INTENT: Understanding God's True Purpose in Creating a World of Grandeur and Beauty by Paul J. Taylor

ISBN (Print): 9781736140505
ISBN (eBook): 9781736140512
LCCN: 2020922534

Cover and interior designed by Ellie Searl, Publishista®

Millennium Works Publishing, Antioch, CA

To my wife, L. Patricia Taylor
My son Christopher P. Taylor and his wife, Jill R. Taylor
My daughter Gia P. Taylor
My chosen daughter Elia Uriarti

My grandchildren
Christal P. Taylor, Autumn M. Taylor, Jamela Kemp, and
James C. Taylor

My Parents
The Late Deacon Paul J. Sr., and Missionary Ida Taylor
Mother Ethel D. Glosson

CONTENTS

ACKNOWLEDGMENTS

THANK YOU TO THE FOLLOWING for your love, support, and prayers:

My siblings and their family
The late James H. Taylor
The Late Assist. State Supervisor Mary E. Tyler
and Administrator Willie F. Tyler
The late Samuel L. Taylor
Joann Taylor
The late William S. Taylor
Diane D. and Bobby Dobbins
Patricia L. Taylor
John I. Taylor
Donald J. and Juliette Taylor
Michael A. and Bridgett Taylor
Bishop Donald E. Green
Pastor Joe L. Nobles
Dr. Anthony Williams
Rev. Hurmon Hamilton

Dr. Horace Sheppard Jr.
Pastor James Parks
Pastor Phil Green
Pastor Roderick Gittens
Pastor Joe Taybron
Dr. Samuel Huddleston
Chaplain Earl Smith
Dr. Stanley Long
Rev. Joe Oliver
Pastor James Withers
Bishop Jerry W. Macklin
Bishop Luther Blackwell
Rev. Allen Belton
Pastor Michael B. Bell
The late Pastor William Pennington
Mr. Bobby Allen (A dear friend and military buddy)
San Francisco Christian Center Family
Victory Temple C. O. G. I. C. Family
Antioch Christian Center Family
Maranatha Christian Center Family

FOREWORD

WHAT WAS IT THAT GOT your attention when you chose to read this book? Was it the title or the graphic design? If it was the title, you are right in the camp with the rest of us. Beyond the debate between evolution and intelligent design, we find ourselves wondering what God had in mind when He decided to bring time and physical life into existence. The answer, of course, may only come at the consummation of all things. I don't think that we will get any answers to this question on this side of time.

The Bible paints a very beautiful and interesting picture of God and His magnificent handiwork. And from that picture I believe we can begin to know something about His intentions for creation.

Some people have accused me of wanting to go too deep into these kinds of biblical matters. But I think that going deep is the thing that keeps us from living a superficial or shallow Christian lifestyle. There ends up being too much "me" in my faith and not enough of God in it. The Bible is about God; it's about Jesus Christ from Genesis to Revelation.

Yes, we play a very integral role, but it's not about us. It's about Him and His love, mercy, and grace on display for both human and spirit beings to see.

The psalmist had it right when he wrote, "O LORD, our Lord, your majestic name fills the earth! Your glory is higher than the heavens. … When I look at the night sky and see the work of your fingers—the moon and the stars you set in place. … O LORD, our Lord, your majestic name fills the earth!" (Psalm 8:1, 3, 9 NLT).

INTRODUCTION

THE WORD *GENESIS* MEANS ORIGINS, beginnings, or source. In the Bible book of Genesis, we see the source or beginnings of the world, humanity, relationships, community, responsibility, and the concepts of rest, sin, and redemption. And, in each of these areas, God has a specific expectation and intent.

Author Julie Ackerman Link said that most of what goes on in the universe we never see. That there are many things that are too small or move too fast or slow for us to see. Our limited ability to see the awesome and intricate details of things in the physical world reminds us that our ability to see and understand what's happening in the spiritual realm is equally limited.

The Bible teaches us that God is at work behind the scenes doing more wonderful things than we can begin to imagine. He allows us to see that which needs to be seen and hides from us that which is not necessary to be seen at this time. But that leaves us with a lot of questions. At the same time, it causes us to come up with lots of speculations and assumptions about

Scripture and spiritual matters that lead to confusion and even conflict because we are not used to living with the mysteries of God.

We see in the book of Genesis the historical account of the origins of life on earth—the creation of nature and animal and human life. We also see the fall of mankind, the effects and impact of sin, and the plan of salvation as announced by God.

On display—in Genesis and in the rest of the Bible as well—is God's love, His justice, mercy, grace, and power to redeem that which was lost. And in the book of Revelation, we see God's power to restore what was lost back to its original perfection.

I've been working in the helping profession for most of my adult life. I've served as a therapeutic counselor to children, teens, and adults—individuals and families. I've provided mediation services to corporations and communities of people. I've done community organizing; worked with men and women reentering society from incarceration; facilitated support groups; taught Bible classes; preached sermons; visited people in hospitals, jails, and prisons, and all of them have this in common: like all the rest of us, they too have been hurt at some point by the evils of this world. We all have been shamed at one time or another. We all have been made to feel guilt, fear, and anger. We've all been touched by trouble and the vicissitudes of life. And that's because we all have been born into a broken world.

However, I rejoice at the fact that God is not going to leave us with this broken world. We have a joyous world in which to live just ahead of us.

In the meantime, though, I have a concern for all these types of people:

- Christians, believers, and followers of Jesus who hear good preaching/teaching on a weekly basis but still live as though they are not saved
- People who consider themselves to be seekers and are only getting parts of the story
- People who know about God but have not committed themselves to a right relationship with Him
- People who have not or have not been allowed to study God's written Word as contained in the Bible
- People who have Bibles in their homes that are collecting dust
- People who believe we should ignore the Old Testament and regulate our lives and behavior according to the New Testament only

A very dear preacher friend of mine expressed to me his frustration with having preached and been a teacher to his congregation for thirty years, yet there seemed to have been no significant change in their behaviors or lifestyles. It was not that they were committing gross sins or anything like that. Rather, it seemed that there was no significant difference between his church members' response to life's vicissitudes and those in the outside world.

In thinking about my friend's frustration, I began to wonder if people were not taking advantage of the whole Bible for guidance and inspiration. Could it be that people of all types have resigned themselves to a life that's not too different from the lives of the characters of the Bible that we find in the pages of Genesis chapter 3 all the way to Jude verse 25? Did people ever consider that it's possible, even in this broken world, to live life according to what God intended in chapter 2 of Genesis and the consummation of all things in the book of Revelation? Trust me, I am not talking about perfection or being right at every turn. Rather, I'm talking about living life according to the blessings God laid out for His Creation and that's contained in Jesus Christ, His Son.

I hope to inspire you, my readers, to understand what took place in the life and times of the people that are recorded in Genesis chapter 3 to Jude verse 25 but allow Genesis chapters 1 and 2 and Revelation to be your vision for life on earth.

Chapter 1: That I Might Know Him!

"Don't let the wise brag of their wisdom. Don't let heroes brag of their exploits. Don't let the rich brag of their riches. If you brag, brag of this and this only: that you understand and know me. I'm God, and I act in loyal love. I do what's right and set things right and fair, and delight in those who do the same things. These are my trademarks."

—Jeremiah 9:23–24 The Message Bible

BOASTING OR BRAGGING IS A verbal kind of showing off. We all boast or brag about something at one time or other. It's in our nature. We brag about things like our favorite sports team, the high school or college we attended, or degrees we have. We also brag about personal achievements and the achievements of our children or other family members. I've heard people make big deals of their jobs, careers, and the number of figures on their paychecks. Then, there are those of us who owned muscle cars in the sixties and seventies—we not only brag about them but the story gets more glamorous with the number of times we talk about our experiences. And don't we love to name-drop. We want people to know whose shoulders we rubbed against over the years.

As obscure as my life has been, I've met and personally talked with some very famous people. However, I am mindful to not use them to bolster myself to some kind of importance.

There is an unending list of things we boast about in our lives. But this great ancient truth from the pen of the prophet Jeremiah tells us that *to know God* is the highest achievement to which any human being could ascend.

My friend, what's your perception of God? I know that some people have this image of God, that He is this big tyrant sitting in heaven waiting to judge people and pounce on them with curses at the least mistakes they make. How unfortunate this concept of the Creator exists in their minds. I believe the Bible when I read that God keeps no record of our deeds, as He has forgiven us, and we are His children. I don't believe God keeps a list of our misdeeds and then uses it to add to the charges against us each time we mess up. As humans, we keep such a record and do not hesitate to bring it out when there are disagreements between us. A lot of couples are famous for this kind of thing. However, God knew we were going to blow it time and time again before He created us (I'll talk more about this a little later in the book).

At the same time, God is not some deity laying back, distant, hands off, or one who refuses to get involved in our affairs. He disproved that notion when He spoke with the prophet Moses about the plight of the children of Israel, who were slaves in Egypt at the time.

In Exodus 3:7, He said to Moses, "I have surely seen the affliction of my people who are in Egypt and have given heed to their cry because of their taskmasters, for I am aware of their sufferings. So, I have come down to deliver them from the power of the Egyptians" (NASB). He sees, He takes heed, He's aware of the situation, and He takes action on our behalf. We verify this with the apostle Paul's letter to the Roman believers. Paul said, "And we know that God causes everything to work together for the good of those who love God and are called according to His purpose for them" (Rom. 8:28 NLT). He's involved even when it doesn't seem that He is. As a Father, He rejoices with us. He suffers when we suffer. He weeps when we weep. He's brokenhearted when our hearts are broken. He identifies with us at every turn in our lives.

The real problem as I see it is that most people, especially of this post-modern generation, have a distorted perspective about God because they know so little about Him. There's lot of confusion out there about His intentions for His creation because people don't know Him as He would like people to know Him.

The book of Genesis tells us a lot about the God who created and loved His creation to the point where He would not give up on it even when things went terribly wrong with it. He had a plan for His creation then, and His plan is still good for us today.

I know you love God as much as I do, and like so many others, we long to know Him and really understand His ways. People wrestle with questions like "Why am I here?" We often ask ourselves, "What is my purpose for being on earth?" We ask these questions in an effort to assure ourselves that there is meaning and significance to our living.

Curtis Kittrell, senior pastor at Faith Mission Church in Temple, Oklahoma, said, "Wherever groups of people are gathered you can observe behaviors revealing a universal 'search for significance.' The drive for significance seems to be a part of our genetic strain." In other words, we want to be somebody.

You may remember some years ago Reverend Jesse Jackson recited, "I am Somebody!" The phrase came from a poem written in the 1950s by Reverend William Holmes Borders Sr. The poem was often recited by Reverend Jackson and used as part of PUSH-Excel, a program designed to motivate young African Americans and students of color to realize they have value as people.

Quite often, but not always, underprivileged and marginalized people struggle with low self-esteem and possibly self-hatred. In having a healthier concept of self, people are able to be better citizens and more productive in their living.

I personally don't see anything wrong with wanting to be somebody or wanting to be great. I am concerned, however, with why a person wants to be great and how he or she goes about becoming a person of significance and greatness. In my opinion, our value and worth do not come from anything on earth or what we do in this world. Rather, our sense of value, worth, and significance comes from the One who created us. They come from the One who said that He has loved us with an everlasting love (Jer. 31:3) and with loving-kindness has drawn us to a relationship with Him.

I have talked with people who say that they know their purpose in life. They seem to have a clear handle on why they exist in the world. Then there are others still seeking answers. Nevertheless, I venture to say that all of us want to know something more about this mysterious God, this Creator who has revealed Himself to us through His Son, Jesus, the Christ of God.

It's one thing to know our purpose in life, which can be understood as resulting from things like our giftedness, talents, skills, passion, education and training, prompting of the Holy Spirit, and interactions with people. But knowing and understanding God and His intent for us takes things to another level.

Understanding what's going on, why we are here, what it all means, and what we are to do as a result of our being here cannot be truly comprehended by looking through the lens of religion and religious activity. This, I believe, is a great problem. It's a problem because we cannot see things the way God sees them if we are trying to understand God by looking at life as it is and human beings the way they are.

A few years ago, I had a television broadcast entitled *See It as God Sees It.* The program was about encouraging people to try to see and live life on earth as God had intended and determined that we were to do. I believed then and still believe now that to really understand and appreciate what God has done, we do well to have heaven's perspective of life under the sun rather than earth's perspective of life under the sun.

My quest on this part of life's journey is to focus more on how God sees things and what He wanted from creation and the people He created. And that is why I'm encouraging as many people as I can to look past the religious thing and embrace the "real" thing. I say this because I believe organized religion as we know and practice it has hijacked real Christianity. There is, in my opinion, too much culture in the church and not enough church in the culture. Living this life is a difficult proposition at best. People are living under all kinds of chaotic situations and circumstances. Jesus Christ is the answer even if they don't believe it. Their unbelief does not stop us from extending to them Christ's love and mercy. I run into people who are looking for the "essential," that one significant thing in life. What is the most important thing?

Here, I am looking to King Solomon for an answer to that question. I believe that Solomon has been misunderstood in terms of his relationship with God and his research about life under the sun. Did he really walk away from God and give in to a life of pleasure-seeking, materialism, folly, and gaining much riches? What if we take a look at Solomon's experience as recorded in the Book of Ecclesiastes? Have you ever thought about it this way? King David, Solomon's father, had intentions of building the temple of God, a place of permanent worship for the people of Israel. However, God had a different plan for temple-building in mind. God used David to conquer the enemy nations around Israel, giving Solomon and the people forty years of peace so that they could build His temple of worship and sacrifice. Forty years is how long it took Solomon and the people to complete the temple. King David resigned himself to gathering all the resources for the temple building, and he and the people of Israel donated money and staged everything for the building project before he died (1 Chronicles chapters 28–29).

Then the people built the temple of God under the leadership of King Solomon. When the temple was finished, Solomon prayed, spoke to the people, and dedicated the temple to God. Sometime later God appeared to Solomon and gave him the opportunity to make any request he desired. Instead of asking for riches, fame, or revenge on his enemies, Solomon asked God for wisdom that he may administrate and govern God's great people. You see, Solomon placed a high value on the people and his responsibility to lead them as their king. His request pleased God, and God gave him everything he didn't ask for (riches, fame, and peace) but also made him the wisest man ever to live aside from God's own Son, Jesus Christ.

Solomon had no wars to fight or enemies to subdue. He was super-rich and famous. People came from all over the known world to visit and talk with him. He was not some idle monarch sitting on the throne with nothing to do.

Some years ago, when I was pastoring a new church group in the San Francisco Bay Area, I got a telephone call from my niece, who lived in Atlanta, Georgia. She and her family wanted to relocate to California. She wanted to live with my wife and me for a while until they could get on their feet. She confided that her father, who was living in Michigan at the time, told her to reach out to me because I wasn't doing anything anyway. Me, a pastor with nothing to do! Believe that?

I said to my wife that my dear brother has no clue what it takes to be a pastor and what all a pastor has to do in a week's time. Being a pastor, husband, father, and leader of people is no small task. Being a king and leader of a nation of people is no small task either. Yet I could not help wondering what an observer and thinker like Solomon would do in the larger scheme of things, especially when he might have had time to reflect on his day or week. Why not do research? he might have been thinking. Why not engage in the discovery of life under the sun for the common man?

I am not sure how Solomon conducted his research. I don't know whether his findings were the result of actual physical indulgence or whether his knowledge and conclusions were the result of revelation knowledge, as in the case with the apostle

Paul in the New Testament. I am not sure. It is likely that Solomon might have interviewed people, received reports from them, and relied on intense observation and his heavenly gift of wisdom to reach the conclusions he wrote about.

At any rate, Solomon was very familiar with the privileges of the rich and famous. He knew what life was like for people of his status, but what about poor and working-class people? What might life be like and what is the most important thing in life for everyday people? He said, "I set my mind to seek and explore by wisdom concerning all that has been done under heaven. It is a grievous task which God has given to the sons of men to be afflicted with" (Eccl. 1:13 NASB).

He tested the futility of pleasure and possessions. He tested the futility of labor. He examined oppression and people's attitude toward God. He thought about the craziness of greed and gaining riches. He examined attitudes toward authority and doing good in life. He looked into the foolishness and silliness of people's behavior. I believe that after years of observing, contemplating, and pondering the plight of earth's people apart from God, Solomon came to a certain conclusion about life. Upon completion of his research, Solomon concluded that life under the sun without God is a futile, meaningless, and empty way of living. So, he said, "Remember also your Creator in the days of your youth" (Eccl. 12:1 NASB). In other words, remember your God, honor Him, and live your life on this earth under his leadership, starting as early in this life as you can.

It seems reasonable to me to say that Solomon looked at life from an "earth to heaven" perspective and found that living according to such a perspective leaves people with an empty and futile existence. I believe that an "earth to heaven" perspective on life is the thing that leaves many of us with lots of unanswered questions.

Could the solution be that we need a change in the way we view our lives? Would understanding life according to how Moses described it in Genesis 1 and 2 help us in our earthly journey to eternity? I'm suggesting that we try to look at life on earth from heaven's perspective rather than try to understand what God is doing from our perspective.

I wear specially designed eyeglasses because of a condition called "adult strabismus"—I have prisms in the lenses of my glasses. The prisms adjust my focus so that I'm seeing singularly and not double letters or objects. Whether for distance, mid-range, or reading, the prisms make letters, numbers, and other objects singular and clearer. Looking at life from God's perspective is like looking through heaven's prisms to get a clearer and more focused and realistic view of life and the world in which we live.

I know this may be really difficult for us to do, but I believe we can do it. I understand that we have to work hard at keeping our feelings and emotions in check when it comes to things that push our buttons. I fight hard to remember that people are not the enemy and that the real enemy is not flesh and blood. I have to keep in mind that the real enemy comprises the evil rulers and authorities of the unseen world. They are the mighty powers of darkness, the wicked spirits who are skillful at using people to carry out their evil schemes against other people.

You know, I really understand the psalmist of Psalm 73.

> Truly God is good to Israel, to those whose hearts are pure. But as for me, I almost lost my

> footing. My feet were slipping, and I was almost gone. For I envied the proud when I saw them prosper despite their wickedness. They seem to live such painless lives; their bodies are so healthy and strong. They don't have troubles like other people; they're not plagued with problems like everyone else. They wear pride like a jeweled necklace and clothe themselves with cruelty. These fat cats have everything their hearts could ever wish for...Then I went into your sanctuary, O God, and I finally understood the destiny of the wicked. (verses 1–7, 17 NLT)

Like the psalmist, I sometimes have a hard time keeping my anger in check when I see people living in cardboard shacks down the hill from their country's leader, who is living in a mansion. I really have to pray when I see the rich, wealthy, and powerful having a party while people evacuate their homes because of wildfires. I want to scream when I sit in meetings and listen to people make plans to help the so-called marginalized and underserved, knowing full well it's just a game for them. It's hard for me to feel any sense of mercy for someone who is running a human trafficking ring.

While these kinds of people are creating victims, they don't really realize that they are victims themselves of the enemy's scheme to destroy their lives.

How different would our lives be if we were able to see people and life as God sees people and life? How different a life would we live if we lived it as God intended rather than as we inherited it? Is there a way to do that?

Yes, there is, and we will talk about that as we go along on this journey to discover God's divine intent for His Creation.

CHAPTER 2: HE HAS REVEALED HIMSELF TO US!

"In the beginning was the Word and the Word was with God, and the Word was God."

—John 1:1 NASB

THERE ARE ALL KINDS OF beginnings. Beginning a new job, relocating to a new city, the first day of school, or the first day at boot camp in the military are just a few examples of beginnings that are a real challenge. Some beginnings are good ones, and some are not so good. Some are exciting and some not so exciting. Some beginnings are simply horrifying.

I remember studying families and family systems in my clinical psychology classes while enrolled in the master's program at our local university. And later the idea of family beginnings became an integral part of the work I did with pre-marriage counseling. At that time the idea of marriage dealt with the concept of a traditional nuclear family that started with a man and a woman joining together in a lifelong relationship. And although the concept of family has dramatically changed over the course of time, the general principles that determined whether the marriage had a good or bad beginning is still valid.

A good beginning to family was characterized by two people who were mentally and emotionally mature coming together regardless of their age in a covenant relationship. They may have been young but were basically prepared for the marriage relationship. In working couples, I saw two people from what I call well-adjusted families coming together to be wedded. The young man and the young woman seemed to have benefited from positive parenting, good role-modeling when it came to raising children, as well as good support from relatives, church, and community. Along with this, their families were considered to be open family systems, which meant that the family did not have to protect its secrets (for example: alcoholism, drug addiction, or family violence) from the scrutiny of the outside world. Let's be clear—although there were good families characterized by good and positive relationship, they were not necessarily perfect.

Through the years, I've witnessed some bad beginnings to the marriage relationship. Sometimes I encountered two people who may have done what I characterize as an escape from their families of origin. In this case, rather than being prepared and properly launched from the family, these unfortunate souls jumped ship and made a great escape.

When I use the term "escape," I'm saying that the young adults may have been victims of violence, abuse, or neglect and may not have been properly supported by the family. There may have been chronic interpersonal conflict between members of the family. There may have been unhealthy attachments among the members.

A seventeen-year-old daughter may have jumped ship and gotten married just to get away from her smothering, overbearing, and controlling mother. A four-year-old son may have been removed from his home due to drugs, crime, and neglect, only to bounce back and forth between one foster home to another and now at eighteen decides to get married. A lack of stability, being conflicted emotionally, and having been exposed to negative influences may have a negative impact on his approach to marriage.

Motives for marriage among escapees, for the most part, are questionable at best. Add to this is the possibility of being mentally and emotionally immature. The two people may have been heavily influenced by negative role models and had learned how to be together in destructive ways. People coming out of closed family systems due to alcoholism, abuse, or violence come with emotional and psychological baggage and have a lot of issues to work through. This is not to say that all children coming from negative or closed family systems are damaged in such ways as not to be able to establish good loving and positive relationships. It is not to say that they can't have a good beginning. I'm simply saying that adult children who escaped their families of origin (closed family systems) may not have been properly prepared for launching and are more likely to enter other adult relationships with distorted ideas as to how things should go. They tend to have unrealistic expectations and behave in negative ways that are counterproductive to getting their needs met. Adult children who escape in such a way may not be able to meet the needs of their mates. And may I say that this holds true for both Christians and non-Christians alike. It's equally true for religious people and those who do not embrace any religious faith at all.

We see in the book of Genesis a picture of not only a good beginning but a great one. That glorious beginning was loaded with unlimited opportunities and possibilities. All the ingredients needed for a fabulous life was there for this first couple. They were set up to live abundant lives on this earth. Adam and Eve were created to serve God's purpose. They were created to involve themselves in His plan for heaven and earth, space, time, and matter. The first couple had opportunity to partner with the Lord, interact with Him, and serve Him in a limitless and boundless fashion. I can't begin to imagine what life would be like if they had stayed true to God. I wonder how different or how much better would our living be if we had had opportunity to live our lives by God's intent as recorded in the first two chapters of Genesis.

What If …?

Imagine for a moment what our human existence would be like if Adam and Eve had resisted and rejected the trickery of the serpent? I've had conversations with many people about the idea of life before the "fall" of mankind, and they sort of dismiss the idea because it's a "utopian" concept. They can't imagine living a life absent of crime, chaos, and catastrophic events. Life as we know it now is as far as their minds will allow them to go.

The problem here is that so many people are too entrenched in our current fallen-world lifestyle. We have been subjugated to the life of good and evil inherited from our fore parents. I realize we can't change what happened before, but through Christ we have opportunity and vision about true life from the Father as recorded in Genesis chapters 1 and 2. I also realize that there is no way I can begin to tell you what life might have been like if sin had not entered into the world. But I can speculate about what might have been by having us look at the opposite of what did happen.

What if there was no such thing as sin existing in people? What if Adam and Eve had fully trusted and stayed loyal to God? What if they continued to live in a state of innocence? This brings to mind the first murder case in the Bible. Cain might not have been so competitive and emotionally out of control to the point of taking his frustration out on his younger brother if he understood God's ways. Did he, Cain, know anything about God's character? He might not have been so downcast and asking the question that so many of us ask at times: Does God care? We often ask the question when we hear of a drunk driver escaping an accident unharmed while the sober victim is seriously hurt or dies. Or like the psalmist who almost lost footing, giving up on God when he saw the arrogant and the wicked prospering while the righteous suffered all kinds of injustices.

Does God care? Habakkuk the prophet wrestled with the same question. He saw the people of Judah in their struggles. Wickedness and injustice were running rampant (Hab. 1:1–4). He was confused and asked God when would He set things right. God told Habakkuk that He used the Chaldeans, who were notoriously cruel people, as the means to correct the people of Judah. The key for Habakkuk was that he may not have understood God's ways, but he could move forward by trusting God's character. He learned to look at his circumstances from the perspective of God's justice, mercy, and truth. Habakkuk concluded that the Sovereign God was his strength, that He made his feet like the sure-footed deer, enabling him to tread on the heights of the mountains.

If Cain had had such a perspective, he might not have been so jealous and envious of Abel and his offering to God. He might have understood that the rejection of his offering had nothing to do with the offering that his brother brought the Lord. He would have learned that God weighs the intent and motive of the heart. Instead of learning such a valuable lesson, Cain followed the pattern of his parents. In the case of his parents, when called to account for their disobedient act, Cain's father Adam blamed his wife Eve for their sinful choice. When God questioned Eve, she blamed the serpent for what happened. The bottom line is neither of his parents took responsibility for their actions. Cain, too, failed to take responsibility for his substandard sacrificial offering to God. He put the blame on his brother, Abel, and eliminated him in a murderous act. An emotionally and mentally healthier Cain would not have committed such an act. He would not have been possessed with an out-of-control anger, which was the product of the sinful nature he inherited from his parents.

It is possible that people might have called on the name of the Lord and lived for Him, as did Enoch, who the Bible said walked with God three hundred years and was taken by God. Some commentators, therefore, say God took his life (maybe while asleep) so he didn't "see" (experience) death. Hebrews 11:5 referencing Enoch says he was taken, and the Greek word used means removed, changed, taken, turned. He did not "see" death (Gr: *horeo*), which means to see with the eyes or the mind, to experience or take heed. In other words, Enoch was changed from life to sleep (death) without having to experience the pain of the transition. All are asleep in the grave until Christ calls them to come out.

Enoch doesn't get a whole lot of biblical press as one of the heroes of faith. What we know about him comes from Genesis 5:21–24. He was the offspring of Jared; whose lineage reaches back to Adam. At the ripe old age of sixty-five, he had a son named Methuselah. The heroic part of Enoch's life is that he walked faithfully with God in a corrupt culture. He was obedient and delighted in communing with the Lord God.

Imagine: the world would have been filled with people like Enoch. People who spoke the same language, people who had respect for one another, people who, even though they believed differently, would have possessed different ideas and opinions and taken different positions on the issues yet lived in harmony and unity.

Imagine a world where all people speak a common language, allowing them to communicate, gain understanding, and enjoy what I call positive prosocial relationships. Imagine also that if God's intent had prevailed with Adam and Eve, we would never have had the "Tower of Babel problem."

There's a story about two men who were questioned as to what they were building together. One said that he was building a garage. The other said that he was building a cathedral. The next day only one man was seen building the walls of the garage. He was asked about his fellow worker, to which he replied that his coworker had gotten fired. What was the reason for his firing? The man said that his coworker had insisted on building a cathedral instead of a garage. The fired worker insisted on building what he wanted instead of what his employer wanted. He wanted to do something he was not authorized to do.

This is similar to what happened on the ancient worksite of Babel. A group of people decided they would build a city and a tower that would reach to the heavens and unite their world (Gen. 11:4). But God did not want them working on a grand self-centered plan based on the idea that they could rise to the heights of God and solve all their own problems. So, He came down, stopped the project, scattered the people "over all the earth," and gave them different languages (verses 8–9). Mart Dehaan said that God wanted people to see Him as the solution to their problems, and He revealed His plans for them to Abraham (Gen. 12:1–3). Through the faith of Abraham and his descendants, He would show the world how to look for a city "whose architect and builder is God (Heb. 11:8–10). "Our faith," says Dehaan, "does not rise out of our own dreams and solutions. The foundation of faith is in God alone and what He can do in and through us."

At the same time, I believe the language confusion created communications problems, competition, and distrust resulting in alienation and separation, classism, racism, and other social problems. People thumbed their nose at God and lived as though He didn't exist. Would there have been conflict or wars between nations and peoples if the Babel incident hadn't happened? I don't know.

A friend of mine said that he thought we would live a boring life if there were no conflict, competition, or wars. To which I replied, "If conflict is so good and capable of producing so many positive things, then why do we spend so much time trying to resolve conflict? Why do we spend so much money putting diplomatic meetings together in an effort to strike peace accords if wars kept us from being bored? In resolving conflict, aren't we really trying to bring about peace and good relations?" I personally believe we will never reach utopia in this world without Christ and His eternal reign. I believe people who think that perfect peace would be boring are the type of people that have become so accustomed to conflict, chaos, trouble, danger, and destruction that they can't imagine anything different.

Let's go a little further with this train of thought. Instead of living in peace and harmony as God had intended from the beginning, people thumbed their nose at God and lived as though He did not exist. As a result of this, many groups of people experienced dreadful and traumatic treatment at the hands of ruthless and dangerous leaders. One such leader was Adolf Hitler whose master plan was to colonize Central and Eastern Europe, which necessitated genocide and ethnic cleansing on a vast scale throughout occupied European territories. His ultimate goal in launching World War II was to establish an Aryan Empire from Germany to the Ural Mountains of Russia and beyond. As a result of Hitler's diabolical plan, some six million Jewish people were sent to their deaths in Nazi concentration camps during the period of 1933–1945.

According to a report from History Vault, at the beginning of the 1830s, nearly 125,000 Native Americans lived on millions of acres of land in George, Tennessee, Alabama, North Carolina, and Florida—land their ancestors had occupied and cultivated for generations. By the end of the decade, very few natives remained anywhere in the southeastern United States. Working on behalf of white settlers who wanted to grow cotton on the Indians' land, the federal government forced them to leave their homelands and walk hundreds of miles to a specially designated "Indian Territory" across the Mississippi River. The difficult and sometimes deadly journey was known as the Trail of Tears.

My primary care doctor, with whom I often have inspiring conversations about life, gave me a book entitled *The Rape of Nanking* by Iris Chang. It's a book about the Japanese army invading the city of Nanking, and within weeks more than 300,000 Chinese civilians and soldiers were systematically raped, tortured, and murdered—a death toll exceeding that of the atomic blasts of Hiroshima and Nagasaki combined.

An article written by Thomas Lewis in the 2005 Encyclopedia Britannica tells us of the transatlantic slave trade that included the transportation of approximate ten to twelve million African people across the Atlantic Ocean to the Americas from the sixteenth to the nineteenth century. Lewis writes that the shipment of slaves was part of a three-stage deal specifying arms, textiles, and wine to be shipped from Europe to Africa, slaves from Africa to the Americas, and sugar and coffee from the Americas to Europe.

I read another article pertaining to slavery and its impact on black people entitled "An American Tragedy: The Legacy of Slavery Lingers in Our Cities' Ghettos," by Glenn C. Loury (March 1, 1998). Loury notes that the thing most often denied is that life in America's ghettos is a race problem. He said that the plight of the underclass is not rightly seen as another (albeit severe) instance of economic inequality, American style. He said that the people who lived in the ghettos were a people apart, susceptible to stereotyping, stigmatized for their cultural styles, isolated socially, and experiencing an internalized sense of helplessness and despair, with limited access to communal networks of mutual assistance. In a word, what we have here is a people whose ancestry and culture were taken away, flooded with drugs and alcohol, and left to develop a subculture where they were viewed as being historically criminal. The inhabitants of ghetto life were thought to be shamelessly immoral, prone to violence, and intellectually inadequate. They were frequently the objects of public ridicule. Loury further says that it doesn't take an enormous power of perception to see how this degradation relates to the shameful history of black-white race relations in this country. However, in spite of slavery and its long-lasting effects, most black people in this country can be heard proclaiming, "God is good" with a response of, "All the time!"

I don't believe that any of these atrocities I've cited here were God's doing but rather the acts of wicked and evil men who did not believe they would ever have to answer for their misdeeds.

I could go on and on with this line of thinking, but suffice it to say, things would most likely have been drastically different—and I might add "for the better"—if our first dad and mom had made a better choice.

One of the big problems for most people, from the dawn of humanity and continuing today—many Christians included—is that we are all pretty much stuck in the reality of chapter 3 of Genesis. In other words, our lives are characterized by life in the rest of the Scriptures spanning all the way to Jude verse 25. We are stuck on self, and because of this we are self-focused and self-centered; we struggle with deception in the mind and conflict in our emotions. We try to understand life and live directed by a mind that has been darkened by sin and spiritually disconnected from God.

The apostle Paul wrote in Romans 8:7 that a mind set on the "flesh" is one that's hostile toward God. A hostile mind does not subject itself to the law of God nor has the power or the will to do so. We behave badly because of distorted beliefs and a lack of knowledge. We ruin good relationships through poor decision-making and unwise choices. We try to live life on our own terms instead of on God's terms. We think we know what's best for ourselves and that we don't need God. Oh, how wrong that is! "Let God be true and every man a liar" (Rom. 3:4 NKJV).

I believe God created us with the intent that we live a high-quality life. For that reason, I think He intended for all of us to thrive and live a full life. I believe God wanted us to enjoy the beauty and benefits of His creative work.

I'm a visual type of person, so the scenes of nature are fascinating to me. I enjoy looking at and admiring things like the snow-capped mountains, beautiful sunrises and sunsets, great vast oceans and seas, the stars at night, forests and trees, and rivers and streams. I have an appreciation for the manmade structures and various inventions like airplanes, ships, and fast cars. And then, of course, there are the animals—those of the wild as well as domesticated. I've admired them up close as in zoos as well as on safari, and the only shots I took were with my camera.

The entrance of sin and sinful human behavior profoundly and negatively affected our quality of life. Our great struggle in life is a result of having been born in sin and fashioned in what King David called "iniquity" (Ps. 51:5 KJV). Therefore, we are sin-conscious and sin-oriented people. Our proclivity is to sin first without thinking.

One Christmas holiday my wife, my granddaughter, and I were invited to a friend's house for dinner. It wasn't long after we had arrived that I got a vivid picture of how innate sin is in us. My granddaughter, about age two at the time, wanted a piece of candy that was in a bowl on the coffee table. She first asked me if she could have some candy, and like all fathers and grandfathers, I told her to go ask her grandmother "Nana." Of course, Nana said no.

Faced with the dilemma of satisfying her desire for that candy and the prohibitive rule of her grandmother, she tried to use a creative strategy to get to the candy. Looking directly at me as I sat on the couch in front of the coffee table, my two-year-old grandbaby put her hands behind her back and proceeded to back up to the table. I pretended to look away, and she grabbed a couple of pieces of candy and went into another room. I called her back, and after an intense interrogation just short of "waterboarding," she confessed her sin and put the candy back into the dish. After reasoning together and getting an understanding, I let her put a piece of candy in her pocket for later.

But it occurred to me after talking with my wife and later with her mother and father, we agreed that no one had really taught her thievery. It seemed to have been an automatic response to rebel against our rule to not get candy and eat it before dinner. It seems to me that we, as people, sin and do wrong automatically but have to be taught and trained how to do right and be righteous people. Maybe it's because, as I mentioned earlier, of what King David said in Psalm 51: "Behold, I was brought forth in iniquity, and in sin my mother conceived me." The Message Bible puts a little bit differently: "You're the One I've violated, and you've seen it all, seen the full extent of my evil. You have all the facts before you; whatever you decide about me is fair. I've been out of step with you for a long time; in the wrong since before I was born" (verses 4–5). To borrow a line from a popular song: "I was born this way."

You see, we inherited a sin nature from our first parents (Adam and Eve). We became tethered to sin, but thanks to God He didn't leave us that way.

Jesus, the promised Savior and Deliverer, came to this earth, lived a sinless life, died on a cross, and was raised from the dead for our salvation. He walked this earth and lived before people as an obedient son to the Father. He is our pattern. That's why the apostle Paul's letter to the church at Ephesus was written to encourage them to live a life imitating Christ. He said, "Follow God's example in everything you do, because you are his dear children. Live a life filled with love for others following the example of Christ, who loved you and gave himself as a sacrifice to take away your sins. And God was pleased because that sacrifice was like sweet perfume to him." (Ephesians 5:1, 2 NLT).

Chapter 3: The Living One

"In the beginning God . . ."

—Genesis 1:1a

WHAT A GREAT DECLARATION! IT is the declaration of all declarations: "In the beginning, God!" It all began with Him. He is before, He is during, and He is after this span we call time. He is eternal. Not only does it all begin with Him, it's all about Him. Here is a thought: it's not about us; it's about Him. It's about His love, His mercy, His grace, His sovereignty, and His severity.

Would you agree with me that there is so much to discover about God? John said about Jesus that it would be impossible to document all He did while here on earth—that the world itself would not be able to contain the books that would be written about Him. (John 21:25).

In his book *Knowing God*, J. I. Packer points out six great realities about God:

- He is the unchanging and unchangeable God.
- His life does not change; He is from all eternity (Psalm 93:2). Created things have a beginning and an ending—not so with God.
- God's character does not change. "Every good thing given, and every perfect gift is from above, coming down from Father of lights, with whom there is no variation or shifting shadow." (James 1:17 NASB)
- God's truth does not change.
- God's ways do not change.
- God's purposes do not change. Balaam told Balak in Numbers 23:19 that "God is not a man, that He should lie, nor a son of man that he should repent." Then Balaam asked Balak a question: "Has He purposed a thing, and will He not do it? Or has He spoken, and will He not make it good?" (NASB)

Here is a brief description of what Scripture says about who God is and what He does. It has been said, and quite often, that there are a lot of people, especially believers, who are trying to live for God without knowing Him. It's one thing to know *about* God, but it is altogether another thing to experience and know Him. The Bible makes these facts clear:

- God is the Master and Majestic Lord. He is our total authority!
- He is more powerful than any false god and is distinct and separate from all that exists!
- He is sovereign, all-powerful, all-knowing, and is everywhere at all times!
- He is the Beginning and the End!
- He works His purposes throughout all the ages!
- He gives strength to the weary, knows us and all our troubles, and no problem is too big for Him to handle!
- He is the all-sufficient source of all of our blessings and meets all our needs!
- God never changes, His promises never fail, He is faithful, and He provides!
- God sets us apart as a chosen people, a royal priesthood, holy unto Himself, a people of His own!
- He cleanses our sin and helps us mature!
- He gives us victory against the flesh, the world, and the Devil!

Packer also said that the greatest task any person could ever undertake is to engage in the discovery of God—paying attention to His name, nature, person, work, doings, and existence.

In the late eighties, I attended a university to complete my master's program in clinical psychology. In one of my classes, I learned how to create a genogram. A genogram is a three-generational pictorial presentation of a family. It goes beyond the traditional family tree in that it includes a lot more information about the family and family dynamics. Learning how to develop a genogram led me to become interested in my own family on both sides. Like so many others, I wanted to learn about my roots, background, and family history. I think most of us want to know about our origins and the impact it may have on our present and future. I find that there is a lot of pride in learning about our lineage and heritage, which helps us to appreciate our place in the world and know that we are not second-class or some "oh-by-the-way" inhabitants on this planet.

Randall W. Yonkers notes that regardless of our lineage, heritage, gender, race/ethnicity, education, or position in life, our glorious origin is found in God Himself. "In recounting the genealogy of Jesus," says Yonkers, Luke concludes the list with this striking passage: "The son of Enosh, the son of Seth, the son of Adam, the son of God" (Luke 3:38 NKJV). We originated from God and belong to Him by both creation and redemption. This is the sure basis for true human worth, meaning, and destiny. It is also the sure basis for unity and communion with God and with one another. Although as humans we are different, living in a diverse world, we all find our unity in God our Creator.

Another reminder that it's about God came from a story I heard about a couple who took their little daughter on a tour of a concert hall to give her exposure to the environment of symphony music. They went into the auditorium to take a look around. The orchestra had just finished rehearsing and was about to take a break. The little girl saw the big concert grand piano on stage and ran up to play her favorite song.

Settling down at the piano, the little girl began to tinker with the keys, playing her little tune. She could only play a few bars of the song's melody. As she played her tune, a master concert pianist came in. On hearing what the little girl was playing, he went to the stage and with his left hand played the lower accompaniment to the song. Then he wrapped himself around the little girl and with his right hand began to play some keys that accentuated the music in the upper range of keys. The little girl's parents were amazed at the sound that came from the stage. What had begun as a feeble attempt to play a simple little tune now sounded like a masterpiece played by a seasoned professional. The master pianist had added to the little girl's effort what only he knew was needed to make the song sound the way it was intended to sound.

In the same way we tinker with life, and God comes along, envelops us, and makes our life into what He intends it to be. He is the One who completes us. Yes, it is about Him!

Think about the apostle John on the isle of Patmos and his encounter with the glorified Jesus and the Holy Spirit. In chapters 4 and 5 of the book of Revelation, John gives us a picture of worship of God as it's done in heaven. This is important because it sets the tone for what we need to consider from this point on. John saw the door to the great throne room of God that had opened. He heard a voice that invited him to come up the stairs and see for himself what things were like in there. Immediately he was engulfed by God's Spirit, which was the only way he'd be able to comprehend what he was about to see and experience.

In the room, John saw something on the throne that seemed impossible to describe. In other words, he didn't have words to adequately describe the glorious reality present before him. How would he attempt to describe what he was seeing? How would he write about it? What words could he use to convey his experience to his readers? Maybe John thought back on the high priest, his garments, and the precious stones that adorned the priestly ephod. Using the names of the precious stones would somehow give an understandable message to the people of the majesty, magnificence, and greatness of God.

John said that the One seated on the throne was like jasper (a clear brilliant diamond-type stone) and carnelian. Carnelian is a powerfully warm and cheerful stone that is rich in color. It is both an energy booster and stabilizer that increases the energy flow in any space in a calm kind of way. Carnelian, in the hands of its holder is said to feel warm and inspire an inner sense of security. Likewise, jasper is said to produce the same effect in people. This to me sounds like our God and the impact His Spirit has on us, wouldn't you say?

The glow surrounding the throne was bowed in shape with a halo effect described as emerald-green in color. At that moment, twenty-four holy leaders dressed in white with gold crowns on their heads bowed before the throne, then cast their crowns to the floor. John said that from the throne came flashes of lightning and rumbling peals of thunder, and in front of the throne were seven blazing lamps. He was told that the seven blazing lamps were the seven spirits of God. The floor leading up to the throne looked like a sea of glass that was as clear as crystal. Present and around the throne were four living creatures whose bodies were covered with eyes in front and in back.

Keep in mind that I don't have space or time to give you a full explanation about the creatures and the various objects contained in these chapters. John said that one of the creatures had the appearance of a lion, another an ox, another a man, and the final one an eagle. Each had six wings with eyes all around and under their wings. The creatures continuously proclaimed day and night, "Holy, Holy, Holy is the Lord God Almighty, who was, and is, and is to come" (Rev. 4:8 NIV).

Then John said that the living creatures ascribed glory and honor, and gave thanks, to the Eternal One seated on the throne. They worshipped Him saying, "You are worthy, our Lord and God, to receive glory and honor, and power, for you created all things, and by your will they were created and have their being" (verses 9–11).

This was worship at its absolute purest. This was "high praise!" It was worship, my friend, that could not be found anywhere else in creation and certainly not on earth. Scripture doesn't say, but I imagine there were thousands of angels and other creatures present at this worship service. This was pure worship because the Living One is worthy of worship.

In light of all this, I have a concern. My concern has to do with this present American culture, which seem to be headed toward a complete disrespectful and irreverent attitude toward God. The Living God, our Creator, must be revered and respected at all times—especially by those who claim to know and follow Him. I believe the church, Christ's body, in this country are like fish who are swimming downstream with this present-day culture instead of swimming upstream as a counterculture. We have become too religious and too worldly oriented in our beliefs and practices. There is too much of the world in the church and too little of the church in the world!

When it comes to the Living One, my concern rings true because of what I believe to be a gross mistake on the part of any human being. Some people are irreverent toward God because they lack understanding. Others are irreverent because they choose to be so. Romans 1:20–21 tells us, "Since the creation of the world His [God's] invisible attributes, His eternal power and divine nature, been clearly seen, being understood through what has been made, so they [people] are without excuse. For even though they knew God, they did not honor Him God or give thanks, but they became futile in their speculations, and their foolish hearts became darkened" (NASB).

I share this with you, my readers, because I believe there are many people acting in irreverent ways toward God due to a lack of understanding of Him rather than just simply choosing to be irreverent.

In spite of the controversy surrounding him, Chinese Christian preacher Witness Lee said adeptly, "Every genuine Christian should have a living relationship with the living God. A genuine Christian interacts with the living God every day and has a living relationship with God because he lives in God and lets God live in him." I believe that it was God's intent, from the beginning, that we live in Him and allow Him to live in and through us

People ask, why is God called the Living God? I say that He is called the Living God because He is the God of the "now." He is the "I am" who is always present because He is eternal, existing outside of time. Unlike His creation, He didn't need anyone to give Him life.

My heart and mind are moved to revere and respect Him because He is the source of life and He has made it possible for us to know Him and make Him known.

I'll close with a few statements about God from an essay written by Robert I. Waggoner, on the website Biblical Theism. Waggoner says that only God has life in Himself (John 5:26) and only God can give life to others. He says that the Living One is the true God who is alive, in contrast to false gods of idolatry (Acts 14:15; 2 Cor. 6:16; 1 Thess. 1:9), which are dead (Ps. 115:3-8; Isa. 44:9–20; Jer. 10:8–10, 14). God listens. He listened to Hannah (1 Sam. 1:11–28); He listened to Solomon (1 Ki. 3:5–14), and He listened to Hezekiah (2 Ki. 19:15–36; Isa. 37:15–17). Waggoner also said that God spoke. He spoke to Adam (Gen. 2:16–17), to Abraham (Gen. 12:1–3), and to Moses (Exodus 3:4).

God listened and spoke to these faithful people in ancient times. He listens and speaks to us today, through His risen Son, Jesus, the Christ of God. Through His written Word, through the prompting of His Holy Spirit, and through our personal experiences with Him, we hear His small, still, but powerful voice.

CHAPTER 4: SOMETHING OUT OF NOTHING

"God created the heavens and the earth."
—Genesis 1:1

GOD CREATED! I'M INTRIGUED BY the word *created*. The Hebrew word is *bara* and is always used to refer to the work of God. Only God can create—that is, call into existence that which had no prior existence.

As Isaac Watts wrote in his famous song: "I sing the mighty power of God that made the mountains rise, that spread the flowing seas abroad, and built the lofty skies."

When I think about calling things into existence that are not, I want to laugh and cry at the same time because many believers have been misled with false ideas stemming from the passage in Romans 4:17, in which the apostle Paul says, "Abraham believed in the God who brings the dead back to life and who creates new things out of nothing." (Rom. 4:17 NLT) Some interpret and apply the verse to our human ability, supposing that we have the power to speak things into our life experience. I believe that we should use positive and encouraging words and stay away from speaking negatively, but we can't by our words make things happen for us by merely speaking of them. I also understand that our words have power. But we don't create; we are created. We just can't speak things into existence.

I am so sorry that so many of us have been misled in this way. It should be obvious to you by now that calling things into existence that did not exist before doesn't work. This is a power God reserved for Himself. And He certainly did not give it to us to be used in the way people do today. It should also be obvious to all of us that we don't have such power because we're still in the same old rut and predicament we've been in for the last six thousand years or more. Trust me, I would love to call a few dollars into existence to get rid of my present debt. I would love to speak to my bad heart condition and make it go away. I believe we should think and speak in positive ways whenever possible. But to have some level of super faith so as to speak to those things that are not as though they were is a power we have not been granted.

"In the beginning, God created" says all we really need to know about the origins of life. But how did He do it? Everyone wants to know that, wouldn't you? There's danger, however, in asking such a question. The danger for many of us is that we won't believe unless we can know and understand how God did it. We want to know by what means God created His heavens and earth. I've met many people who, like the disciple Thomas, refuse to believe until they see proof. Thomas refused to believe Jesus had been raised from the dead until he saw Jesus's scars (Jo. 20:24–29).

Many Christians are stuck on a treadmill, as it were, waiting on God to give them all the details before they take on a ministry assignment. It's as if they're saying, "Tell me and I'll go," when God is saying, "Go and I'll tell you." Although I might not understand how God did it, I just believe that the all-wise and all-powerful One is who He says He is and does what He says He can do. Creation is a mystery that does not need to be solved; creation is a blessing that needs to be enjoyed.

Spiros Zodhiates, general editor of the Hebrew-Greek Study Bible, said, "God of His own free will and by His absolute power called the whole universe into being, evoking into existence that which was previously non-existent."

The prophet Isaiah wrote, "God, the Lord, created the heavens and stretched them out. He created the earth and everything in it. He gives breath to everyone, life to everyone who walks the earth." (Isaiah 42:5 NLT)

The shepherd boy who became Israel's king must have thought extensively about God and His creative work. You remember David. The prophet Samuel paid David's family a visit one day to fulfill his mission from God. That mission was to anoint young David to be king over Israel. God had rejected King Saul and made the determination that David would be His choice as king for His people, the Israelites.

Imagine the things that might have been going through that young man's mind just prior to his anointing to be king. David had been charged with shepherding his family's flock. His responsibility took him away from the house. He spent most of his time out in the fields with the sheep, leading them to green pastures and water. Now along comes the prophet Samuel, and David is summoned to come back to the house. When he arrives, he finds an unusual event taking place. Here his parents and his brothers are standing around the man of God. The ruddy, handsome shepherd boy with the pleasant eyes is made to stand facing the prophet. Samuel takes the olive oil and pours it on David's head. Scripture records that the Spirit of the Lord came mightily upon David from that day on.

It was after his calling and anointing that David began to reflect on the awesome majestic God of creation. Can't you just hear him? The sheep heard him. "O Lord, our Lord, your majestic name fills the earth! Your glory is higher than the heavens" (Ps. 8:1 NLT). I ask you: How did David know this? How was he so informed as to be able to say this or even write it down as a historical record?

I don't believe this was the first time he had lain under the darkened skies observing the moon, stars, and asteroids with comets shooting across the heavens. He pondered and thought about the nature life God had created. He declared, "When I look at the night sky and see the work of your fingers—the moon and the stars you have set in place …" I have to ask the question he asked: "What are mortals that you should think of us, mere humans that you should care for us?" (Ps. 8:3–4 NLT). David continued with his thoughts on God's creative work concerning human life, declaring, "For you made them only a little lower than God and crowned them with glory and honor… You have taught children and infants to tell of your strength, silencing your enemies and all who oppose you" (verses 5, 2) David does not only recognize God's creative work concerning nature life and human life but turns to focus on animal life as well. He says, "The sheep and the cattle and all the wild animals, the birds in the sky, the fish in the sea, and everything that swims the ocean currents" were put under the rule and authority of the human beings God created (verse 8). David expresses wonder when he concludes his psalm by saying, "O Lord, our Lord, your majestic name fills the earth."

He is lauding the great creative work of God as captured in the book of Genesis.

Psalm 8 is special to me because it reminds me of God's majestic power, glory, and splendor. I look at the heavens and nature and marvel at His magnificent creative touch.

I'm always observing people everywhere I go. My wife laughs at me sometimes when we go to a restaurant, the grocery store, or shopping mall because I'm scanning the crowd and checking out the people and how they are behaving. She often asks, when she catches me in full radar mode, "What do you see now?"

What is it that I see in Psalm 8, you ask? I see David praising God for His majestic work. He uses the weak to conquer the mighty. He entrusted His creation to the dominion of people. Each person is insignificant compared to the breathtaking work of creation, yet God cares for every person on the planet. My friend, I encourage you to continue to trust God and look to Him. You can trust that He knows, cares for, and loves you dearly. You might be overwhelmed with whatever is going on in your life. It may seem like your situation will never change. Perhaps it may seem as though God has abandoned you.

He has not. He loves you. He cares about you. There is no trouble or dire circumstances any of us face that God isn't actively involved with. God told Moses, when speaking about the children of Israel, "I have indeed seen the misery of my people in Egypt. I have heard them crying out because of their slave drivers, and I am concerned about their suffering. So, I have come down to rescue them from the hand of the Egyptians and to bring them up out of that land into a good and spacious land, a land flowing with milk and honey" (Ex. 3:7–8 NIV).

Psalm 136, written during the reign of King Solomon, also gives testimony to the creative work of our Lord. Psalm 148 and Proverbs 8:22–31 are testaments to God's handiwork as well.

The apostle Paul, preaching in Athens, says this: "He is the God who made the world and everything in it. Since he is Lord of heaven and earth, he doesn't live in man-made temples, and human hands can't serve his needs—for he has no needs. He himself gives life and breath to everything, and he satisfies every need. From one man he created all the nations throughout the whole earth. He decided beforehand when they should rise and fall, and he determined their boundaries" (Acts 17:24–26 NLT).

Dr. Henry Morris says in his book *The Genesis Record: A Scientific and Devotional Commentary on the Book of Beginnings* that the usages of the word *create*, here in Genesis 1:1, informs us that, at this point, the physical universe was spoken into existence by God. It had no existence prior to this primeval creative act of God. God alone is infinite and eternal. God is also omnipotent, so that it is possible for Him to call the universe into being. It is impossible for us to comprehend fully the concept of an eternal God calling into existence a self-existing universe. So, the choice comes down to an eternal God creating versus a self-originating body of matter. The latter is impossible if the present scientific law of cause and effect is valid, since random particles of matter could not, by themselves, generate a complex order of the universe. A personal God is the only adequate Cause to produce such effects.

The writer of Hebrews wrote, "Every house is built by someone, but the builder of all things is God" (Heb. 3:4 NASB). And in Revelation 4:11, the apostle John recorded what the twenty-four elders said: "You are worthy, our Lord and God, to receive glory and honor and power, for you created all things, and by your will they were created and have their being" (NIV).

I find great value in pondering and meditating on these passages of Scripture because they set the tone for how I view God and my relationship to Him. I believe if we are to ever live as God desires us to live, we must see life and all creation as God sees it.

Seeing Life, the Way God Sees It

I mentioned this before and repeat it here. Another of our problems is we try to understand and comprehend what God does and is doing from an anthropological perspective. In other words, we look from earth up to heaven in an effort to understand our God and the life we've inherited rather than looking from heaven down to earth to understand the work and intentions of God.

Let me expand on this idea a little more. Our life view and view of God and His ways must be within the context of the Creator's intent for His creation. If our worldview and view of God is not informed in this way, we will continue to miss the mark. Missing the mark explains why people have such a hard time understanding, believing in, and trusting the very God who first trusted them. The apostle Paul wrote to the Corinthians about having the mind of Christ (1 Cor. 2:16). We need to possess the full spectrum of Christ's mind—if that's possible for finite people to do. I don't think we will ever understand *why* God does what He does, but we can see and ponder *what* He has done. Knowing what God has done is enough for us to figure out what we need to do. He made something out of nothing and then He turned nothing into something.

I like to think of it in terms of a saying that I use in some of my sermons. There's an old cliché that goes like this: God stepped out of nowhere, unto nothing, and created everything. I don't take credit for originating the saying, but you get the idea. It's a word picture of the awesome wisdom and power of Almighty God.

So, what am I getting at here? For the past twenty-five years I've been trying to look at life and things from God's perspective versus from my human perspective. It's not an easy thing to do given the finiteness of my human mind. The beauty is that I don't have to do it. Thank God for faith. As I said before, I don't have to try to figure out why God does what He does or prove anything about Him. He is! He does! "And without faith it is impossible to please God, because anyone who comes to him must believe that he exists and that he rewards those who earnestly seek him." (Heb. 11:6 NIV)

I believe He is who He says He is and does what He says He can and will do. But am I capable of seeing it as He sees it? Can I really view life from His perspective? I don't know but I'm going to try. Seeing it as He sees it and trying to view existence from His perspective has me taking a fresh look at Scripture and imagining what life might be like as opposed to the way life is now. This does not negate Christ and the work of redemption. Thank God that He made provisions to restore us to a right relationship with Him while we were lost and so far from Him.

But what would life had been like if our first parents had remained obedient and faithful to the Lord God and not given in to their lustful desires?

God's will, His purpose, and His divine intent for Adam and Eve is the same as it is for us. All of creation and everything that exists does so because of his will, purpose, and divine intent.

Joseph's Destiny

Think about the life and experience of Joseph, son of Jacob and Rachel. Here is a good example of what God intends for a person's life contrasted to what that person might believe is his own purpose for being here on this planet.

Joseph had a dream. It was a dream of greatness. He dreamt that one day he would be in a very powerful position and his family would have to come to him, subjugate themselves, and depend on him for their survival. Okay, let's go back a few scenes. Along with his older brothers, Joseph was tasked with feeding the family's flock of sheep. However, his undercover work was that of a spy. One day he brought back to his father a bad report about his brothers (Genesis chapter 37). Now, understand that they were already jealous of the boy because of the favoritism shown by his father.

There was so much going on in this family from a psychological, emotional, and relational standpoint that it would take another book to describe it all. The brothers hated Joseph. There was a lot of conflict not only between the brothers but also between their mothers and father. The seeds of discord had been sewn when the mothers competed for Jacob's time and affection. There was Rachel, Joseph's mother, who got all the print, press releases, and interviews. There was

Leah, her older sister, who was not as attractive or popular. Leah couldn't even get a footnote mention on the back page of the *Bethel Gazette*. By the way, God had held Rachel back from having children while blessing Leah to give birth to six sons. Rachel was furious. She seemed to have spent a lot of time complaining and nagging Jacob about not having children. It was to the point where Jacob, feeling irritated and agitated, said to her, in effect, "What do you think I can do about it? I'm not God! I've done everything I can. You have to talk to God about this."

Rachel did not know that she was infertile by divine decree. What God's reason was for not allowing her to have children at that point, I do not know. It might have been God's way of evening the score between Leah and her; God does champion the underdog. Rachel was the loved one, the favorite, and the chosen one of Jacob. God allowed Leah to give birth to four sons, one of which was Judah, from whom Jesus Christ would descend. Nevertheless, Rachel spent a lot of time complaining and nagging Jacob about not having children. Eventually, God allowed Rachel to give birth to two sons, Joseph and Benjamin.

At the young age of seventeen, Joseph had two dreams from God. I say this because not all dreams are from God. Some dreams originate from a combination of mental, psychological, and emotional (subconscious) sources. But Joseph's dreams from God contained God's purpose, plan, and destiny for Joseph's life and the nation of Israel. By the way, contrary to the popular notion espoused by sports announcers and writers, no one controls their own destiny. There was no way for Joseph to control anything about his experience except how he responded to every challenge he faced. God was in control of Joseph's life. God was orchestrating and working things out so that Joseph would end up in a place I call "God's Intent: Joseph's Destiny." And that was as prime minister and administrator of Egypt, second only to the Pharaoh, the ruler.

In other words, it was God who called Joseph to his destiny. It was God who kept the young man and encouraged him every step of the way. Scripture records that it was God who was with Joseph. It was God who gave the young man favor with authority. It was God who gave Joseph the knowledge of and ability to interpret dreams. And it was God who gave Joseph the wisdom and ability to act appropriately in the different situations he faced on his journey. Wow, God is so amazing! He used the actions and behaviors of this young man to serve His purpose and save an entire nation of people.

The Lord's purpose and will is not coercive or forced on His creation. He loves and respects His creation, and He takes their freedom seriously. God's sovereign rule is expressed in terms of faithfulness and patience.

As a teacher and preacher, I've invited nonbelievers to trust God for their lives. I've also heard other pastors and ministers use the same concept of 'trust' in their invitation to have people repent of their sins, receive Christ, and ask Him to be their Savior, Lord, and leader of their lives.

In thinking about this notion, however, I'm not sure trusting God is the right way to make such an appeal. What do I mean? God is not the one who needs to be questioned as to His trustworthiness. God does not lie, His word is true, He keeps His promises, and nothing is impossible for Him. Therefore, we don't have to worry about God failing or going back on His word. We are the ones who should be in question. We are the inconsistent, flaky ones that are prone to go back on our word. So, the question for me is not whether I trust God for my life. Rather, the question is, can God trust me with His life in me?

It seems to me that God put His reputation on the line when He created the heavens, earth, and people. His reputation was on the line when He put humans in charge of everything. And we can see from the beginning how that worked out. Time after time people failed to keep their charge. The question is, can God trust us to follow His lead, obey His word, get to know Him, and make Him known?

The apostle Paul in Romans 1:20 says, "For ever since the world was created, people have seen the earth and sky. Through everything God has made, they can clearly see his invisible qualities—his eternal power and divine nature. So, they have no excuse for not knowing God" (NLT). God speaks to creation and makes His intent and desire known. He calls His creation to faithfully respond through joyful obedience. Can God trust you, my friend, to respond to Him in faithful and joyful obedience?

In the presence of everything happening in the world, we have not been turned loose on our own. Nor have we been abandoned. However, at the same time, we have not been given free rein to exert our own inclinations. God is in control.

CHAPTER 5: UNFURNISHED AND UNFINISHED

"The earth was empty, a formless mass cloaked in darkness."

—Genesis 1:2 NLT

PHILIP YANCEY WROTE AN ENTRY entitle "The Good Earth" in the November 11, 2017 installment of *Our Daily Bread*:

> While orbiting the moon in 1968, Apollo 8 astronaut Bill Anders described the crew's close-up view of the moonscape. He called it "a foreboding horizon … a stark and unappetizing-looking place." Then the crew took turns reading to a watching world from Genesis 1:1–10. After Commander Frank Borman finished verse 10, "And God saw that it was good," he signed off with, "God bless all of you, all of you on the good earth."
>
> The opening chapter of the Bible insists on two facts: Creation is God's work. The phrase "and God said …" beats in cadence all the way

> through the chapter. The entire magnificent world we live in is the product of His creative work. All that follows in the Bible reinforces the message of Genesis 1: behind all of history there is God.
>
> Secondly, creation is good. Another sentence tolls softly, like a bell, throughout this chapter. "And God saw that it was good." Much has changed since that first moment of creation. Genesis 1 describes the world as God wanted it, before any spoiling. Whatever beauty we sense in nature today is a faint echo of the pristine state God created. The Apollo 8 astronauts saw Earth as a brightly colored ball hanging alone in space. It looked at once awesomely beautiful and fragile. It looked like the view from Genesis 1.

In the beginning, planet Earth was a ball of physical matter covered by water, and the passage says that it was empty.

Two years after my wife and I were married, we bought a house in a little city just south of San Francisco, California, called Daly City. In my mind, it was just right. It had three bedrooms with one and a half baths. Yes, it was perfect with lots of space for the three of us—my wife, me, and our son. My daughter had not been conceived yet, so the house had adequate space and well-situated rooms, but it was empty. It had not been furnished. By the way, an unfurnished house led me to discover my wife's gift of shopping. And shop we did! By the time we had finished our shopping, our little house was not only just right, it was fully furnished and complete.

The heavens and the earth were just right but not complete. Heaven and earth were perfect, but at the beginning of beginnings they were not fully furnished. There were no stars, galaxies, or planets. On earth, dry land had not appeared. There were no designated oceans, seas, lakes, or rivers. There were no mountains or valleys. There was no desert or rainforest; no cloud formations; no trees, flowers, or shrubs. The earth was just a ball of matter covered by water.

To be void meant that heaven and earth were empty and lacking something. There were no life forms. No nature life, animal life, or human life. The great ball of water and empty space were cloaked in darkness. There was no light. There were no heavenly bodies—no sun, moon, or stars.

Here's a thought. I discovered that God works well in the darkness. In the book *The Valley of Vision: A Collection of Puritan Prayers & Devotions* (edited by Arthur Bennett), I found a section that was written about the distance between a sinful man and his holy God. The man said that God brought him to the valley of vision. The man felted hemmed in by mountains of sin but that, in spite of his predicament, he still beheld the glory of God. Also being aware of his sinful deeds, he still had hope. He said that the stars could be seen from the deepest wells, and the deeper the wells, the brighter the stars shone. Finally, the sinful man prayed that God would let him find the Lord's light in his darkness and God's glory in his valley. The article goes on to say that although sin creates distance between God and us, we can look up from the lowest points in our lives and see Him—His holiness, goodness, and grace. If we turn away from our sin and confess it to God, He will forgive us.

Many times, over the course of the years, I've been in dark places. It was in the dark places that I saw the beauty, grandeur, and power of God on display. He's not afraid of the darkness in us. He is the One who brings light into darkness. God paints some of His greatest masterpieces in the darkness of our lives.

The earth was empty, formless, and cloaked in darkness. What a description of humanity. What a picture of the lives of human beings who reject God and choose to live a lifestyle of sin. They may be famous and successful in life. They may live a long life and prosper, but spiritually these well-meaning beings are really living an existence of separation, desolation, and obscurity. They really live empty lives, void of anything meaningful. In other words, their lives are empty and void of the life of God. They live a life cloaked in darkness. The sinner's life is a life without order, without substance, meaningless and useless for God's purposes, although God can and does use useless people from time to time to accomplish certain things. Overall, however, the life of a person disconnected from God is a life that is unfurnished and unfinished.

There are people from all walks of life who are concerned about being a good person. You probably know some of them. Maybe you have family members who perhaps made that same declaration. I know you've heard statements like "I'm a good person; I don't hurt anybody." Then there are other people who strive to do good things in an effort to balance the scales against the bad that they do.

I can tell you, folks, it does not work that way—at least not according to the Bible. According to the Bible, good or bad does not matter; whether you do better than bad doesn't matter. The fact is Christ died for everyone. He died for the good and the bad, the rich and the poor. He was the sacrifice that saved all of us.

When it comes to missing the mark, we're all in the same boat. "All have sinned; we all fall short of God's glorious standard"

(Rom. 3:23 NLT). Both good people and bad people need the salvation Christ brings. Both good and badly need the life of God residing in their hearts transforming, growing, and maturing us to Christlike-ness. God gave his Son so that we can experience rebirth and live the way He intended us to live from the beginning. The fact is, as I said before, Christ died for all of us no matter how or in whatever state we were born. Our lives without Him are unfinished. Not only are they unfinished but greatly lacking the furnishings that makes them complete.

Our lives without the actions and involvement of Christ Jesus, by the Holy Spirit, have something missing. What might be missing, you ask? Missing from our lives is the presence, peace, and power of God. The apostle John wrote, "All those who love me," said Jesus, "will do what I say. My Father will love them, and we will come to them and make our home with each of them" (Jo. 14:23 NLT). A house filled with the presence of God is a fully furnished house. Think about a house in which the furnishings are love, joy, peace, patience, kindness, goodness, faithfulness, gentleness, and self-control. God at home in our hearts is the furnishing we need to be complete. Likewise, the heavens and the earth needed the actions and involvement of the Father, the Son (His Word), and the Holy Spirit to become fully furnished and complete.

Chapter 6: Power Poised for Production!

"And the Spirit of God was hovering over the surface . . ."

—*Genesis 1:2*

GOD'S ALL-POWERFUL SPIRIT WAS at the ready. He not merely an active force, as some have claimed. He is a personality and not an inanimate object. He is the life of God that animates and gives life to people. There is a spirit in man, and the inspiration (Holy Spirit) of the Almighty gives them understanding. He is the power of God who makes things happen as God the Father commands. Besides his active role in the creative process, the Spirit of God can be seen throughout Scripture anointing and gifting people for special service in God's kingdom. He empowers people to do miraculous things, enabling them to give life and bring people back from the dead. And, most of all, He is the soul agent for the transformation of believers. He builds godly character and bears fruit in the lives of followers of the Lord Jesus Christ.

There are more than fifty-one references to the Holy Spirit in the Bible. A study of Him is a book series in and of itself, so we won't try to cover Him here except to identify and study His role in creation.

Let us take a look at the sequence of events. In the beginning God the Father thought, desired, intended, purposed, and planned it. God said—in other words, He spoke. His Word commanded a certain thing to happen. God said, "Let there be …," and the Word (who would later take on humanity) ordered it to happen, and the Holy Spirit, the power of God, brought it to pass. The Father purposed creation; the Son ordered time, space, and matter to come forth; and the Holy Spirit materialized it.

Here is a partial listing of the Holy Spirit's service record (all taken from NKJV):

- He strives with humanity. "And the Lord said, 'My Spirit shall not strive with man forever'" (Gen. 6:3).
- God used his Spirit to expand leadership responsibilities among the people of Israel. To Moses, he said, "Gather to Me seventy men of the elders of Israel. … Then I will come down and talk with you there. I will take of the Spirit that is upon you and will put the same upon them; and they shall bear the burden of the people with you" (Num. 11:16–17).
- He empowers people to live according to the will of God. "I will put my Spirit within you and cause you to walk in My statutes, and you will keep My judgments and do them." (Ezek. 36:27).

- He's the power that produces life. "Now the birth of Jesus Christ was as follows: After his mother Mary was betrothed to Joseph, before they came together, she was found to be with child of the Holy Spirit" (Matt. 1:18).
- Believers are immersed in him for baptism. John the Baptist said, "I indeed baptized you with water, but He will baptize you with the Holy Spirit" (Mark 1:8).
- He speaks to authority through the believer. Jesus said to his disciples, "When they arrest you and deliver you up, do not worry beforehand, or premeditate what you will speak. But whatever is given you in that hour, speak that; for it is not you who speak, but the Holy Spirit" (Mark 13:11).
- He anoints believers for service as He did Jesus prior to his wilderness testing and the beginning of His Galilean ministry. "And the Holy Spirit descended in bodily form like a dove upon Him" (Luke 3:22).
- He empowers believers to witness for Christ. Jesus told his disciples, "You shall receive power when the Holy Spirit has come upon you; and you shall be witnesses to Me in Jerusalem, and in all Judea and Samaria, and to the end part of the earth" (Acts 1:8).
- He is the righteousness, peace, and joy each believer needs. The apostle Paul wrote, "For

the kingdom of God is not eating and drinking, but righteousness and peace and joy in the Holy Spirit" (Rom. 14:17).

- He gives gifts to the church. "But the manifestation of the Spirit is given to each one for the profit of all" (1 Cor. 12:7).
- He brings freedom to God's people. "[God,] who also made us sufficient as ministers of the new covenant, not of the letter but of the Spirit. … Now the Lord is the Spirit; and where the Spirit of the Lord is, there is liberty" (2 Cor. 3:6, 17).
- He is the seal of promise. "In Him you also trusted, after you heard the word of truth, the gospel of your salvation; in whom also, having believed, you were sealed with the Holy Spirit of promise" (Eph. 1:13).
- He gives prophecy. "Now the Spirit expressly says that in latter times some will depart from the faith" (1Tim. 4:1).
- And finally, he enables believers to preach the gospel. "For prophecy never came by the will of man, but holy men of God spoke as they were moved by the Holy Spirit" (2 Pet. 1:21).

Before I move on from here, there are four very important things missing if the Holy Spirit is not present within us:

1. We lose our point of reference. There would be no moral absolutes or objective truths to

rely on. We are left without a moral compass, which is the problem with lots of people in our country. There are no standards, nothing immovable to hold on to in this chaotic world. Our sense of purpose is lost. We are left feeling insignificant in the world.

2. There is a loss of the meaning of life. The late Dr. Billy Graham said, "Life without God is like an unsharpened pencil; it has no point." I think about the millions of people trying to find meaning and significance through other means. But the truth is, every pursuit in life is futile if God is not included.

3. There is no recovery. We are left to die broken, fallen, and never having the opportunity to experience life as God intended.

4. We lose eternity with God. There's no hope beyond the grave.

Creation everywhere was in need of activation. The Spirit of God, who is both omnipresent and omnipotent, was at work in the creation. He moved in the presence of the waters, hovering as a mother hen over her little ones. He energized the universe, setting things in motion as the Father intended.

CHAPTER 7: DAY ONE: THIS LITTLE LIGHT OF MINE

J.authorupda

"Then God said, 'Let there be light,' and there was light. And God saw that the light was good. Then he separated the light from the darkness. God called the light 'day' and the darkness 'night.'"

—Genesis 1:3-5 NLT

THE PHRASE "AND GOD SAID let there be …" occurs at least four times in the first chapter of Genesis. God spoke the words, and whatever He spoke came into existence. What a wonderful proposition to ponder. In the face of all life's challenges, obstacles, and battles, it's thrilling and inspiring to know that God is working things together behind the scenes for our good because we love Him and are called according to His purpose (Rom. 8:28). Creation was God's initiative, and His power was on display when He spoke. Someone once said, "God said it, I believe it, and that settles it."

Before we deal with light, I want to talk about God's Word. John said, "In the beginning was the Word, and the Word was with God and the Word was God. He was with

God in the beginning. … The Word became flesh and made his dwelling among us. We have seen his glory, the glory of the one and only Son, who came from the Father" (John 1:1–2, 14 NIV). From this we know that the God's Word takes human form, becoming flesh. We cannot fully understand how God can be captured or confined to the body of a human being. But God came in human form, a miraculous event we call the "incarnation."

Jesus, the Word made flesh, was the image of the invisible God. By him all things were created things in heaven and on earth, visible and invisible. The Father was pleased to have all the fullness of the Godhead dwell in him. "For in Christ all the fullness of the Deity lives in bodily form" (Col. 2:9 NIV). The reason for that was so that the Word (Jesus, the Son of God) could reconcile all things to His Father.

God's first act in creation was to command light to come forth. The light, at that point, was separate from darkness. The light was different from sunlight or moonlight. The sun and the moon were not created until the fourth day. John said of Jesus, "In him was life, and that life was the light of all mankind" (John 1:4 NIV). The light was personified by Jesus, the Christ, Son of the living God.

John saw light as more than a physical phenomenon of electromagnetic radiation. Light is tied to life, and the source for both is the creating Word of God. It has been said that according to the laws of physical science, all living creatures on the earth depend on the light of the sun, either directly or indirectly. In the same way, spiritually speaking, we need the light that comes from God in order to have life (see John 10:10). The life was personified by Jesus Christ.

Dr. C. I. Scofield does not see Genesis 1:3–5 as an originating creative act of God. Rather, Scofield believes that light was made to appear or become visible. He believes that the sun and moon were created "in the beginning" but were hidden by the clouded expanse because vapor diffuses or blocks light. Light, according to Scofield, came later as the sun appeared in a cloudless sky.

While Scofield's literal interpretation may work where a natural explanation about the sun and moon is needed, it does not work where a spiritual application is necessary. God spoke and light came into being. There was light before there were heavenly bodies such as the sun, moon, and stars. In the book of Revelation, the apostle John writes, "I saw no temple in it," talking about the new heaven, earth, and the city of God, "for the Lord God Almighty and the Lamb are its temple. The city had no need of the sun or of the moon to shine in it, for the glory of God illuminated it. The Lamb is its light. And the nations of those who are saved shall walk in its light" (Rev. 21:22–24 NKJV). Time, at the very moment of creation, was introduced to a reality that eternity had known all along. God is light!

"Let there be light" meant that God, who is light, was on the move enacting in time to give life and meaning to His creation. The Ultimate Light moved to fill the darkness with Himself. Darkness, at that point, was not associated with sin, wickedness, or evil. Rather, darkness was understood to be void, empty, or a situation of nothingness.

The light in Genesis meant that the presence of God was then revealed to time, space, and matter. The light in Revelation means that the presence of God is with the people who commit to Him.

Again, I stress the fact that I do not wish to get entangled in any theological debate over this study and these passages. My only objective is to focus on my responsibility as a worshipper of God and faithful follower of Christ Jesus. The focus being on how I shall live in light of Genesis's description of the divine acts of God in creation. The overriding question for me is, how shall I navigate this journey through life, given the laws of life, my stewardship responsibility, the governance and rule of God, and my relationship with Him and with others?

I came across an excerpt from the book *For Time and Forever: God's Wonderful Plan,* by Dr. Henry Morris, founder and president emeritus of the Institute for Creation Research. I print a portion of that book here by permission because I think it says it best.

> One of the most amazing statements ever made was the assertion of Jesus Christ in the temple in Jerusalem one early morning long ago, speaking to a group of bigoted religionists who were seeking an excuse to condemn Him. This claim immediately brands Him as either a raving lunatic or a conniving charlatan—or— (could it conceivably be true?) as the very Son of God himself! ...
>
> Here is what He said: *"I am the light of the world; he that followeth me shall not walk in darkness but shall have the light of life"* (John 8:12).
>
> A listener may have thought, *But, Sir, it is the mighty sun that illumines the world, not some*

wandering preacher from Galilee like yourself. The sun moving high in the sky provides light so that men do not have to walk around in the dark, so how can you claim to be the sun? The sun does, indeed, make life possible, with its radiant energy causing plants to grow and rivers to flow; it can certainly be said to be "the light of life," but how can you, of all creatures, claim to give life?

"Oh," His followers might reply, "He was just speaking metaphorically. He is the *spiritual* light, giving *spiritual* life, conquering *spiritual* darkness, not really claiming to produce sunlight."

But that's just as bad, isn't it? This country preacher with no formal education and only a motley group of deluded followers! Yet here He is professing to provide the spiritual, as well as moral and intellectual guidance for the whole wide world, when neither He nor His disciples have ever even traveled beyond the borders of Israel! How could this Jesus, from Nazareth, possibly expect anyone to believe *that*?

Yet, for the past two thousand years there have indeed been millions of people from all over this whole wide world who have believed just that, and whose lives have been transformed because of it. Further, not only have individual men and women been transformed; so, have whole societies and cultures. Great educational institutions have been established in His name, as well as hospitals and charities of all kinds, not to mention multiplied thousands of churches and

> helpful ministries in great variety. Nations have been established to serve Him; even the worldwide evil of slavery has been almost abolished.
>
> Most of the founding fathers of science were sincere followers of Jesus, as well as the greatest medical researchers of the past. The Lord Jesus Christ, even though despised by so many of His contemporaries that He was judicially executed in a uniquely cruel manner by their leaders, has indeed been the Light of the World ever since, not only spiritually, but also intellectually and morally. Those who choose to follow Him have not walked in darkness but gladly testify that they have found the Light of life, just as He promised.

We need the light! We need the natural light of the "sun" and we need the spiritual light of the "Son." God knew that on a natural human and physical level we would need light because He created us as non-nocturnal beings. On a spiritual level we need the light of Christ because after Adam and Eve, darkness would be equated with sin. The apostle John said, "In Him was life, and the life was the light of men. And the light shines in the darkness, and the darkness did not comprehend it … That was the true Light which gives light to every man coming into the world" (Jo. 1:4–5, 9 NKJV). And Jesus said in John 8:12, "I am the light of the world. He who follows Me shall not walk in the darkness but have the light of life." The apostle Paul in Ephesians 5:8, 10 (NASB) states, "For you were formerly darkness, but now you are Light in the Lord; walk as children of light … trying to learn what is pleasing to the Lord."

God does not want us to walk in darkness. This kind of darkness makes us like the earth at the beginning of creation. If we walk in darkness, our lives are void and empty, resulting in a state of nothingness and uselessness. We are dead even though we are living. The consequence is that we live this life with no sense of meaning or purpose. We find ourselves useless when it comes to God's intent, purpose, will, and plan for our lives. Therefore, He brings the Light of Jesus Christ into our lives. Christ restores the value and worth of our being that was lost due to the fall of mankind. Because of the light, the path to meaning and purpose becomes clear and easy to traverse.

"Let there be light" was an intentional and purposeful move of God. It was a move unlike any other. It was a move from emptiness to fullness, from primitive darkness to God's marvelous light. This movement took six days, beginning with God speaking and ordering time, space, and matter into existence. The psalmist declared that "By the word of the Lord the heavens were made, the starry host by the breath of his mouth ... For he spoke, and it came to be; he commanded, and it stood firm" (Ps. 33:6, 9 NIV).

Let there be light! God said what He meant and meant what He said. He put His awesome power on display, revealing to us, through this Genesis record, His intention, so that we can trust His goodness, everlasting mercy, and truth that endures to every generation.

"And the evening and the morning were the first day" (Gen. 1:5).

CHAPTER 8: DAY TWO: THE SUPER DOME

"Then God said, 'Let there be an expanse in the midst of the waters, and let it separate the waters from the waters.' God made the expanse and separated the waters which were below the expanse from the waters which were above the expanse, and it was so. God called the expanse heaven."

—Genesis 1:6–8 NASB

AFTER BRINGING LIGHT INTO DARKNESS, our all-powerful Creator proceeded to order both the atmosphere and hydrosphere to come into being. In ordering the firmament to come forth, God was preparing the earth to be able to sustain all forms of life that were yet to be created. Some sources call it the firmament. Others call it the sky, dome, expanse, heaven, or lower heaven. Whatever term used, the waters above are separated from the seas, oceans, lakes, and rivers below.

God began by speaking light into existence, and light would provide for the growth of grasses, plants, and trees, on which the animals as well as humans would depend for food. Humans and animals alike need to breathe. God created a colorless gaseous element we know as the atmosphere. The atmosphere was the firmament or dome that separated the waters below from the waters that were above.

Ancient Israelites believed that the horizon was the boundary where light and darkness met. Human beings could not travel beyond this point to find God since God lives beyond the horizon. They understood the sky to be like a solid bowl or dome set over the earth, and high mountains held up the sky like columns. We find in the book of Job the following verse: "The pillars of heaven tremble and are amazed at His rebuke" (26:11 NASB). The rationale for the sky being a solid bowl or dome was that it was necessary for it to hold back the massive band of water sustained above.

William W. Winter, author of *The Origin of the Universe, Standard Lesson Commentary*, said,

> The word *firmament* may be misleading. God did not call into being something firm, like a glass bowl turned upside down over the earth. The Hebrew word for firmament comes from a verb that means 'to spread out.' As a noun, the word describes an expanse, something spread out. The firmament, therefore, is the space spread out above us, the space into which we look from the earth. At first that space was not very high. It reached out only to the cloud cover that still surrounded the whole earth. Thus, with the creation of the firmament a division was made in the waters that enshrouded the globe.

The ancients described rain and snow as coming through the dome when God opened windows or doors in the sky. Moses wrote the following, speaking of the Great Flood: "The floodgates of the sky were opened. The rain fell upon the earth for forty days and forty nights" (Gen. 7:11 NASB). The psalmist said, "Yet he gave a command to the skies above and opened the doors of the heavens" (Ps. 78:23).

The concept of there being windows or doors in the firmament was also promoted by the prophet Malachi, who wrote to encourage the Israelites to be faithful in their tithing and sacrifices. The people of Israel were supposed to give to the Lord a tenth portion of everything they harvested, along with unblemished animals from their flock and herds. (See Lev. 27:30–33; Num. 18:21–24; Deut. 12:5–19; 14:22–29; and Neh. 13:12.)

"Bring the whole tithe into the storehouse, that there may be food in my house. Test me in this, says the Lord Almighty, "and see if I will not throw open the floodgates of heaven and pour out so much blessing that there will not be room enough to store it" (Mal. 3:10 NIV). From a natural and not a spiritual standpoint we may believe that Malachi was referring to rain, since during his time there was a terrible drought in the land. However, it seems clear that no rain or snow would touch the earth unless God opened the doors or windows of heaven. Thus, the windows or doors were the access points by which blessings flowed from God through the dome, expanse, of firmament to earth.

God's Throne — The Third Heaven

The Waters above the Firmament

The Firmament — The Second Heaven
Sun –Moon – Stars

Earth's Atmosphere — The First Heaven

Earth — Land
Waters on the Surface
Rivers – Lakes – Seas – Oceans

We notice in verse 7 that Moses uses the term God "made" and not God "created." Winters says, "In forming the firmament, God used elements that He had already brought into being." Verse 6 shows us God's purpose for making the firmament, and verse 7 tells us how He fulfilled His purpose. The firmament divided the waters that were above it (clouds) from the waters that were under it (waters on the surface of the earth). With this arrangement God set in motion the processes by which the waters above would condense and fall to earth as rain and the waters on earth's surface (rivers, lakes, seas, and oceans) evaporate into the atmosphere forming a continuous cycle.

When I see the water cycle, I think of the cycle of living through Jesus Christ. He is the Son who gives life. We receive energy from Him through the Holy Spirit, who rains down on us and who is in us as the power from above. He empowers us to provide for and contribute to life—everything God has wired us to do. We recognize God's blessings and in turn pour out our gratitude and praise back up to the Father. Thus, we have the saying, "When the praises go up, the blessings come down." We don't praise Him to get blessings, but we praise Him because we are blessed.

"And there was evening, and there was morning—the second day" (Gen. 1:8 NIV).

Chapter 9: Day Three: This Land is Your Land

"And God said, 'Let the water under the sky be gathered to one place and let dry ground appear.' And it was so. God called the dry ground 'land,' and the gathered waters he called 'seas.' And God saw that it was good. Then God said, 'Let the land produce vegetation: seed-bearing plants and trees on the land that bear fruit with seed in it, according to their various kinds.' And it was so. The land produced vegetation: plants bearing seed according to their kinds and trees bearing fruit with seed in it according to their kinds. And God saw that it was good."

—*Genesis 1:9–12 NIV*

God's creative activity on this third day involved formatting the earth and bringing order into it. He separated the lithosphere (dry land) from the hydrosphere (atmosphere). The waters became earth's oceans, seas, and lakes. We don't know how God separated the waters from dry land except that he ordered it and it was so. Did he raise the land above the surface of the waters? Did he cause the volcanos to erupt until they spilled out lava to the point of breaking the surface of the waters, forming land mass? Or was there such a movement of the tectonic plates that pushed the land upward to form mountains, and between each set of ranges there were low places called valleys? Did he cause other areas on the earth's surface to be depressed, making reservoirs of water?

I learned in my geology class something I found very fascinating. There are places in the ocean—especially in the Pacific Ocean—that are so deep as to have mountains whose peaks are higher than many of the mountain peaks we see on the earth's surface. How did He do it? We don't know. It's both miraculous and a mysterious. In this so-called "need to know" climate, it seems people want to know everything now rather than embrace the mysteries of God.

There don't seem to be too many people who can live with such mysteries. And that's the fundamental question here. Can you live with the mysteries of God? Does your "need to know" drive you to read things into the Bible that are not there because God, through His Holy Spirit, did not prompt His writers to leave us a record of them? There is knowledge that came at a *particular* time (for example: Jesus's teachings, actions, and miracles in the presence of His disciples); knowledge that was revealed at a *later* time (for example: the burning hearts of the two travelers on the road to Emmaus in Luke 24); and knowledge to be revealed at the *end* of time, as the apostle John said in 1 John 3:2, "We know that when Christ appears, we shall be like him, for we will see him just as he is" (NIV). There was knowledge about life, the beginning of life, the world of living, and beliefs and actions of human beings revealed in ancient times. There are scientific discoveries and divine enlightenment for our time. And, in the end, there will be revelation of all truth.

William Winters said, "Nearly three-fourths of the earth's surface is covered with water. If some should think that such a vast expanse of water is wasted area and useless, let them consider that there is a delicate balance between rainfall and the water needs of the earth. With less ocean surface, the lessened evaporation would result in extensive barren, arid wastelands of the earth. God made the proportion just right to serve the needs of man."

Speaking of dry land, what about the rich treasures God stored in the earth all over the globe? I thought about this, and memories of my geology class came flooding in. God really blessed us when He placed all the elements in and on the earth for our benefit. I believe everything and everyone that's a part of the economy of God has value and worth. Nothing of His creation is to be written off, just as nothing in the natural world is without purpose and can be written off.

The gospel according Luke (13:6–9) revealed a people who believed others of their community were worse than themselves and deserving the punishment they were receiving. The suffering groups were non-repenting sinners deemed more guilty than all the others living in Jerusalem. Jesus took the opportunity to teach them that all people were in need of repentance. Then he told them a parable about a fig tree. A man planted a fig tree in his garden, but the tree failed to produce figs. The owner told his gardener that he was going to cut the tree down because it had failed to produce fruit for three consecutive years. "Cut it down," the owner said, but the gardener begged him to give the tree one more year. The gardener was going to cultivate the ground around the tree, fertilize it, and see if it would bear fruit. Hidden in this account is God's intent and expectations for our natural world. Everything created was expected to make its contribution to life and existence.

Charles Boatman asks the question, "Have you ever wondered why God created certain things?" He goes on to say, "The tobacco industry insists their product is good, in spite of the health hazards that statistics suggest are associated with its use by human beings. Yet there is some good in it: tobacco is said to make an effective insecticide! Marijuana has made 'potheads' of many people, but medically supervised dosages have been used to treat glaucoma."

Boatman further says that "in the animal kingdom are many examples of creatures some might consider 'useless.' What good could a spitting, smelly camel be? Desert dwellers know its value: it can go for long periods of time without food or water, and special eyelids enable it to endure sandstorms that stop other beast of burden. … Out of an unorganized mass of material, God brought forth a creation that is repeatedly said to be 'good.' He can also take lives that the world discounts as unattractive and worthless and make of them something beautiful."

I spent six years working with incarcerated and formerly incarcerated men and women returning to Contra Costa County, California. I get different reactions from people when asked what is it that I do. Some are really impressed and supportive of my efforts, while others seem not interested in giving these men and women second and third chances at getting their lives together. At the same time there are reentry persons who are serious about making changes and going forward with their lives in positive ways and others who attempt to take our services and make them a part of their "con" and criminogenic game. Regardless, what's really interesting is I've found some of the most intelligent and talented people ever among the returnees that I worked with. Society may have written them off—locked them up and thrown away the keys. However, I would not want to have locked up and thrown away the key for one of my clients who successfully reunited with his eleven-year-old daughter who went from delinquency and truancy to engagement in her academics and schooling. She also plays drums in her father's church band. God is good, and He has a way of bringing people to good points in their lives.

"There was evening, and there was morning—the third day" (Gen. 1:13 NIV).

Chapter 10: Day Four: Here Comes the Sun

"Then God said, 'Let there be lights in the firmament of the heavens to divide the day from the night; and let them be for signs and seasons, and for days and years: and let them be for lights in the firmament of the heavens to give light on the earth'; and it was so. The God made two great lights: the greater light to rule the day, and the lesser light to rule the night. He made the stars also. God set them in the firmament of the heavens to give light on the earth, and to rule over the day and over the night, and to divide the light from the darkness. And God saw that it was good."

—Genesis 1:14–18 NKJV

HERE WE HAVE THE CREATION and formation of the heavenly bodies. "Then God said …" There are several references in the Psalms that attribute creation of the sun and moon to God. Psalm 74, which is a didactic poem of Asaph's, was written against the backdrop of the fall of Judah to the Babylonians and the destruction of the temple in 586 BC. Psalm 74 was Israel's cry for help and declaration of hope that God would one day deliver them from captivity and restore them to their homeland. In it, the psalmist declares that the day and night belong to God, the maker of the sun, which gives light.

Prior to Psalm 74 and at the time of the Jerusalem temple dedication, King Solomon wrote Psalm 136. The psalm was a call-and-response style or liturgy exalting the Lord's steadfast love. In verses 7–9 (NASB), Solomon was proclaiming God's great works in nature:

> To Him who made the great lights, For His
> lovingkindness is everlasting.
>
> The sun to rule by day, For His lovingkindness is
> everlasting:
>
> The moon and stars to rule by night, For His
> lovingkindness is everlasting.

Then, prior to Psalm 136, David wrote Psalm 19 at the time of his anointing by the prophet Samuel, which is a hymn of praise. David reflects on the glory of God in natural revelation and the glory of the law as God's special revelation, which alone meets man's spiritual needs. Day governed by the sun and night governed by the moon broadcast their silent but eloquent speech declaring the glory of God.

Sunlight is earth's primary source of energy. Ultraviolet light from the sun has antiseptic properties and can be used to sanitize tools and water. I remember a conversation I had with a former church pastor. We'd just come out of the building, and it was raining. I made a comment about the rain. He said to me, "Be thankful—look how God uses the rain to wash away all the germs and filth from the sidewalks and street."

I gleaned from that comment a renewed appreciation for the rain. In like manner sunlight is utilized by the cholesterol in our skin cells to make vitamin D, which enhances the absorption of calcium, iron, magnesium, phosphate, and zinc. Vitamin D helps prevent osteoporosis by strengthening bones.

Not only was the sun created to provide energy to the earth for human health and plant life but to give mankind a way to tell time. The sun rises in the east and sets in the west, giving us an indication of time. The sun also helps with direction and navigation especially when driving, flying, sailing, and even walking. There were several miracles in the Bible involving the sun. Joshua, leading the Israelites in battle against the Amorites, prayed the sun would stand still, which gave them more daytime to defeat the Amorites (Josh. 10:12–15). God used the sun's shadow as a sign of His promise to make King Hezekiah victorious over the king of Assyria (Isa. 38:7–8).

God is the physical source and sustainer of all life on earth. Thanks be to God our Father for the heavenly bodies and the ecosystem of earth that support our earthly living!

"There was evening and there was morning, a fourth day" (Gen. 1:19 NASB).

CHAPTER 11: DAY FIVE: DOVES, RAVENS, GATORS, AND SHARKS

"And God said, 'Let the waters bring forth swarms of living creatures, and let birds fly above the earth across the firmament of the heavens.' So, God created the great sea monsters and every living creature that moves, with which the waters swarm, according to their kinds, and every winged bird according to its kind. And God saw that it was good. God blessed them, saying, 'Be fruitful and multiply and fill the waters in the seas, and let birds multiply on the earth.'"

—*Genesis 1:20–22 RSV*

THE HEAVENS WERE COMPLETED AND fully furnished. The earth, having been called into existence, was now formed and firm. The atmosphere. hydrosphere, lithosphere, and biosphere had been carefully arranged to support plant, animal, and human life. In other words, formation of the solar system and preparation of the land for habitation was completed. The creation of birds, fish, and sea creatures marked the first appearance of conscious life having *nephesh*, a soul. Dr. Morris writes:

> The first introduction of animal life was not a fragile blob of protoplasm that happened to come together in response to electrical discharges over a primeval ocean, as evolutionists believe. Rather, the waters suddenly swarmed *abundantly* with swarming creatures (the waters did not "bring forth," as mistranslated in the Authorize Version). …
>
> In the Biblical sense, plants do not have real life, or soul (or consciousness); but both animal and men do. …
>
> Animal life was not simply "brought forth" from the earth or water, as was true for plant life. The principle of consciousness was not capable of development merely by complex organization of the basic physical elements; and so, it required a new creation. God had created the physical elements of the universe on the first day and here He performed his second act of true creation. "God created great whales, and every living creature that moved." The "living creature" is same as the "living soul," so that this act of creation can be understood as the creation of the entity of conscious life which would henceforth be an integral part of every animate being, including man.

This was part of Dr. Morris's rebuttal of evolutionists' claim that life evolved from protoplasm. However, it is useful to us because, here again, we need to understand that whatever God called into being, it (man, fish, and fowl) had to live and subsist on that from which it had been called. So, we understand that Adam was made from the dust of the earth and it stands to reason that he would be sustained by the food supplies produced by the earth.

"And the evening and the morning were the fifth day" (Gen. 1:23 NKJV).

CHAPTER 12: DAY SIX: A THUNDERING HERD

> *"Then God said, 'Let the earth bring forth the living creatures according to its kind: cattle and creeping thing and beast of the earth, each according to its kind'; and it was so. And God made the beast of the earth according to its kind, the cattle … and everything that creeps upon the earth according to its kind. And God saw that it was good."*
>
> *—Genesis 1:24–25 NIV*

AFTER THE INHABITANTS OF THE hydrosphere and the atmosphere were brought in to occupy the neighborhood, the citizens of the lithosphere and biosphere moved in. The land was stocked with living creatures: cattle, creeping things, and beasts. Some became domesticated and some remained wild and untamed.

In 1991, I was privileged to travel with a group of ministers to Kenya in East Africa. The mission was twofold. First, we were tasked with groundbreaking and dedicating a building to be constructed to serve as an elementary school on the outskirts of Nairobi. Second, each of us had individual responsibilities to fulfill. Some had been assigned to preach and teach at various churches in and around the city. Other ministers led discussion centered on major issues facing different congregational groups from different churches. I was tasked with conflict-resolution responsibilities working with parents and their children who were leaving farm life for a promise of educational opportunities in the schools and university to be built in and around Nairobi.

After weeks of work we were treated to a safari trip to the Masai Mara, Kenya's national game reserve, which butted up against Tanzania's Serengeti National Park. It was very timely because the great migration of animals was taking place at the time. There were gazelles, water buffalos, bucks, zebra, and wildebeest as far as the eye could see. Following them were the predators—lions, cheetahs, and hyenas by land and vultures and other flying creatures by air. We saw hippos, rhinos, and elephants. I could only marvel at God's great creation and handiwork.

In a later chapter I will talk about Adam's responsibility to take care of the land as part of his stewardship duties. But how would he cut the grasses without a lawnmower? How would he trim the trees or cut back the brush without a chainsaw or hedge clippers? Then I remembered the land animals. Wildebeests and gazelles fed on the grasses; giraffes and kudus ate the leaves and shoots; Chimps, monkeys, gorillas, and bucks ate the fruit, nuts, and bamboo shoots; and elephants ate twigs, tree bark, roots, and small plants. These animals—while all may not have been in Adam's immediate area—were workers with Adam, landscaping God's great earthly property. God has a purpose for everything and everyone He created.

The lithosphere teamed with land animals, creatures, and creeping things. And, thus, the biosphere was completed.

Chapter 13: Set Up to Succeed

"Then God said, 'Let Us make man in Our image, according to Our likeness' ... God created man in His own image, in the image of God He created him; male and female He created them."

—Genesis 1:26–27 NIV

PEOPLE HAVE A TENDENCY TO not revere God as I believe they should. I don't particularly care for terms like "the man upstairs" or "the big dodger in the sky." It's disrespectful and brings God down to a human level.

The Bible tells how young David was out in the fields, all alone with his sheep. He saw something special in those night skies as recorded in Psalm 8. David saw God using the weak to conqueror the mighty. He saw God entrusting His creation to the dominion of the human beings He created. David saw the insignificance of people compared to the breathtaking work of creation and yet understood that God cared for every person He created.

Karl Marx said, "Religion is the opium of the people." Marx thought that belief in God was an idea the oppressed embraced to survive the misery of their daily lives. What Marx failed to realize was that Christianity is not a religion. Christianity is a way of life that's highlighted by a personal relationship with Jesus Christ.

Christians know that in all things pertaining to their lives, God is behind the scenes working things together for their good because they love Him, and they have been called according to His purpose for their lives (Rom. 8:28). Marx believed that his social revolution would make things equal among the people to the point they would no longer need to look to God for relief from their sufferings. Charles Boatman wrote:

> To make sure that people realized they did not need God, the heirs of the Bolshevik Revolution in 1917 outlawed God: the Communists wrote His obituary. God no longer existed—Soviet law said so! *However*, most people didn't get the message. Throughout seventy years of Communist rule and suppression of religion, the church survived. And when the Soviet Union collapsed, the church emerged again as a visible, powerful force of life in the lands that once lay behind the "iron curtain." Christianity survived everything the Communists could do to exterminate it for one simple reason: human beings are created to respond to our Maker.

There is a place in us that cannot be filled by anything that exists other than God, our Father. We are made in His image!

Here, in this passage in Psalm 8 we see the first mention of the divine name *Elohim*. Elohim is a declaration of the awesome majesty and omnipotence of God. Dr. Henry Morris says that the "im" ending of the Hebrew word Elohim makes it plural. Elohim can mean "gods" and is so translated in various passages referring to the gods of the heathens. Morris believes that the use of the word *Elohim* in this verse is singular and is the mighty name of God the Creator. In other words, Elohim is a plural name with a singular meaning. Elohim here in Genesis 1 is singular, and the word occurs more than two thousand times in Scripture. It is a "uni-plural" noun, suggesting the uni-plurality of the Godhead. God is one, yet more than one.

Did you know that there are twenty-one names and titles for God in the Bible? And did you know that each name or title has a significant meaning for people who put their faith in Him? Each name and title inform us of God's existence, His power, and His ability to meet our every need. The apostle John in his gospel helps us to understand this fact when he writes that the Word who was God was with God in the beginning, and all things were created by Him (Jo. 1:1). All things continue to exist because of Him. God not only created us, He also created everything we would ever need to live a high-quality life.

Made in His Image

What does it mean to be created or made in God's image? Man was created as a natural physical being with the responsibility to care of a natural physical planet. Adam and Eve were also made in the spiritual and moral likeness of Elohim. Their bodies were formed from the dust of the earth, and life came from the breath of God. Human life is much like nature and animal life. They are natural bodies animated by the breath of God. But Adam is said to have been created in the image of God, which was something not said about the plants, animals, or creatures. Made in God's image seems to go a little further in its conception.

What then is the image of God? Steve Ham, in his article "What Is the Image of God?" says that the image of God has nothing to do with our bodies, experience, or function but rather it's about God's righteous attributes. He uses as his reference Ephesians 4:24, which reads, "Put on the new self, which in the likeness of God has been created in righteousness and holiness of truth." (NASB) Steve also notes Colossians 3:10, which reads, "Put on the new self who is being renewed to a true knowledge according to the image of the One who created him" (NASB). God's image, according to Ham, is an image of righteousness and holiness. For example, God is love and His love is perfect—that is, absolutely complete. We were created to reflect God's love as we make our journey on this earth. God does have, according to Ham, character traits that He does not share with humanity (for example, God is self-existent, omniscient, and omnipresent). But we can still see His shared attributes in humanity today even though they are distorted by sin. We share attributes like love, self-awareness, justice, grace, and mercy, which are distinct from attributes associated with animals.

Made in the image and likeness of God seems to have been a divine enablement to the first couple, empowering them for their impending responsibility to rule and reproduce. And ruling and reproducing is not a calling to be taken lightly, by any means. Please understand that ruling and having dominion is through Jesus Christ. All things were put under His feet (Heb. 2:8).

To Rule like Him!

"And let them rule over the fish of the sea and over the birds of the sky, and over the cattle, and over all the earth, and over every creeping thing that creeps on the earth. … Rule over the fish of the sea and over the birds of the sky and over every living thing that moves on the earth" (Gen. 1:26, 28 NASB).

As God's representatives, mankind was set up to rule the earth. God's purpose in creating man was that he should rule over animal life and caretake nature life. Bible scholar Gordon Wenham wrote:

> Because man is created in God's image, he is king over nature. He rules the world on God's behalf. This is of course no license for the unbridled exploitation and subjugation of nature. Ancient oriental kings were expected to be devoted to the welfare of their subjects, especially the poorest and weakest members of society … By upholding divine principles of law and justice, rulers promoted peace and prosperity for all their subjects. Similarly, mankind is here commissioned to rule nature as a benevolent king, acting as God's representative over them and therefore treating them in the same way as God who created them.

Adam and Eve forfeited that blessed privilege when they sinned and lost their divine enablement to fully do the job.

To Reproduce like Him!

"God blessed them; and God said to them, 'Be fruitful and multiply, and fill the earth, and subdue it; and rule over the fish of the and over the birds of the sky and over every living thing that moves on the earth'" (Gen. 1:28 NASB).

The first thing we see is the power and authority to procreate. Be fruitful, multiply, and fill the earth. This is a mind-boggling privilege. What a powerful blessing we were given to be able to bring a life into this world. The Bible doesn't say that the angels were given this ability. Yet, we humans, made lower than the angels, were blessed with the privilege to procreate and produce life. Okay, the privilege to procreate is one thing, but to fill the earth with our offspring, subdue the earth, and rule? Come on, man, what else do we need?

When God gave Adam and Eve the command to be fruitful, multiply, and fill the earth, his intent for mankind became apparent to me. Just what might have been the Creator's intent for his creation on this matter? Up to the time of this command, God was speaking to a couple who had not yet sinned and was living in what is commonly called a state of innocence. Had the Creator's command been explicitly obeyed and not violated, the earth would be filled with sinless, innocent worshippers of God.

God wanted to entrust His creation to the care of responsible caretakers that would, as time went by, produce additional responsible caretakers. But, of course, we know that sin stepped in, and we missed that mark by mega-miles.

In the book of Malachi, God expressed his displeasure with the men of Israel, who were guilty of breaking faith with the wives of their youth. He said that the men acted treacherously and violently toward their wives, and their actions led to divorce, something He hated (Mal. 2:6). Violence, abuse, mistreatment, and destructive conflict has a powerfully adverse effect on the children. Broken and dysfunctional families made it difficult for children to grow up to love and serve God. Relationship treachery produced a shame-based survival mentality in the children. Children get their perception of God from their parents and significantly important people in their lives. If these influential people are harsh, cruel, and abusive, the children will perceive God to be that way.

Now, don't misunderstand me. There is a difference between being loving, firm, and respectful of the dignity of children as opposed to being harsh, cruel, and abusive toward them. This point is made clear from the apostle Paul's instruction to fathers in the book of Ephesians. I like the way Eugene Peterson says it in the Message Bible: "Fathers, don't exasperate your children by coming down hard on them. Take them by the hand and lead them in the way of the Master" (Eph. 6:2). I believe God-loving, God-serving, people-loving, and people-serving human beings is what the Creator had in mind to populate His earth.

Thrive like Him

"God said, 'Behold, I have given you every plant yielding seed that is on the surface of all the earth, and every tree which has fruit yielding seed; it shall be food for you; and to every beast of the earth and to every bird of the sky and to everything that moves on the earth, which has life, I have given every green plant for food'; And it was so" (Gen.1:29–30 NASB).

God intends for everyone to thrive. His intentions were that we thrive economically, emotionally, physically, relationally, environmentally, morally, and spiritually. God's basic provisions are an essential part of thriving in life; however, I believe that these verses point to or culminate in the Lord's declaration in John's gospel. Jesus said that the thief (the enemy of life) comes to steal, kill, and destroy but that He came to give life—abundantly and for eternity (Jo. 10:10). The food God provided was good for both nourishment and health. Adam and Eve did not lack for anything. They had everything!

I believe God wants us to be successful. His intent from the beginning of time was that His created humans should be successful. Success was His idea, not ours. I believe that in the same way that He set the children of Israel up to succeed when bringing them out of Egypt to the Promised Land, He sets us up to succeed through Jesus Christ, our Promised Land. The Father, through the death and resurrection of His Son, delivered us from sin to righteousness and from darkness to light. The Creator's intent was for his created beings to have dominion and rule in the earth realm. And because Adam sinned, God accomplishes or makes His intention reality through Jesus Christ, the second Adam (1 Cor. 15:47). Our design and destiny were finished before it all began. Our lives, my friends, were finished—completed before we were born. The question we must ask ourselves is this: "Are we going to walk in God's completeness or not?"

The challenge for us is to see life on earth as God sees it and govern ourselves accordingly. After all, God set us up to be successful in all our life's endeavors. The same blessings given to Adam and Eve are also available to us through Christ Jesus our Lord. I believe if the Bible was taken away from us and Genesis chapter 1 was all I had to go on, my faith and trust of Almighty God would not take the slightest hit. It would be enough for me live for God and look to the second coming of Christ.

The circles below tell me everything I need to know about His divine intent for my life. This was the setup for Adam and Eve; it is the setup, through Jesus Christ, for all of us. The big question to ask is, what is your perspective of this life God has given you? Another way of asking this question is, what are you doing with this great gift God has given you?

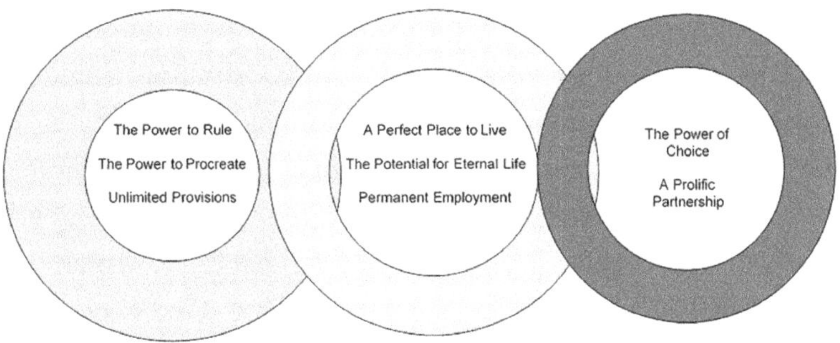

It Was All Good!

"God saw everything that he had made, and behold, it was very good. And there was evening and there was morning, the sixth day" (Gen. 1:31 ESV).

The first parents had the freedom to enjoy life as part of God's family. But they also had to respect the Creator's instructions. They had freedom but were expected to honor His restrictions, and the consequences for disobedience were laid out. If they followed God's instruction, they would enjoy life forever under His care and direction. But if they chose to go their own way, they would suffer and eventually die. With freedom of choice—free will—came responsibility. This is the choice each of us faces today.

While choice offers a measure of freedom, many people struggle with the challenge of living in freedom. Some people believe that freedom comes only from within. They believe that they can use their mental, psychological, and emotional powers to navigate freedom's journey. It's good to be strong and take control, but one must realize it takes more than that to deal with this fallen world and the residue of sin within. The freedom life is a day-to-day battle. There is no room for complacency and living on cruise control. Successful freedom living requires that we develop skills to manage our emotions and not give in to what I hear called "stinking thinking." Successful freedom living is following God's path of righteousness and not the world's path of evil and wickedness.

Here in chapter 1 of Genesis, we see that everything was not only good but very good! And in chapter 2, which is a recapitulation of chapter 1, we see that God's plan for humankind was the enjoyment of the beauty, abundance, and fruitfulness of His creation.

Chapter 14: Day Seven—A Day of Rest

"So, the creation of the heavens and the earth and everything in them was completed. On the seventh day, God had finished his work of creation, so he rested from all his work. And God blessed the seventh day and declared it holy, because it was the day when he rested from all his work of creation."

—Genesis 2:1–3 NLT

GOD'S INTENTION FOR THE WORLD and everything in it is culminated in a Sabbath. The first inhabitants had a perfect place in which to live, all the provisions they would ever need, and a privileged relationship with their Creator.

Creation was magnificently completed. The word *completed* stands out as a declaration for all time. Why did God rest and institute the Sabbath? Because creation was complete, lacking nothing. There was nothing to evolve. Everything that had been created was commanded to reproduce after its own kind. The universe was set to operate according to the laws of nature. Life in the realm of time was ready to function as God, Creator, intended it to do. So, God rested from His work—He ceased from any additional creative work.

He rested! What did it mean for God to rest? How do we reconcile the idea of God resting with the passage in Psalm127:4 that says God never slumbers or sleeps? Also, Jesus said, "My Father keeps working and so do I." (Jo. 5:17). God rested from His work of creating even though He is never at any time weary or tired.

I remember when retail stores closed business on Sundays and holidays. I remember when the unions fought for eight-hour workdays and any hours beyond that would get overtime pay. Many workers were able to sit down to an evening meal with their families, and if they had to work extended hours, it was the exception and not the rule.

Things have changed in recent times with the advances in technology. We hardly get a break from our cell phones, laptops, and notepads. And because of technology it's possible to almost work 24/7. My daughter often works from home for her job. Sometimes she's on a conference call early mornings, working on her laptop during midday, and ends the day on conference calls late into the evenings. Sometimes I think the only thing that would stop her is a rolling power outage.

We've become a society of Uber drivers hauling our kids from the football fields to the soccer fields and from piano lessons to basketball practices. We eat on the run and crash on the couch at night totally exhausted. Another thing that robs us of rest is working overtime to pay for houses that are too big and cars we can't afford to repair or keep up with scheduled maintenance. We become so frustrated by the daily commute to and from work that all we want to do is get home, sit down, and be entertained by the TV. No time to pray because we must sleep fast and get up ready for the next day.

David Egner said, "It seems that we often put ourselves under enormous pressure to succeed and to experience everything we possibly can. When we don't, we can't forgive ourselves for failing to measure up to our own expectations. But is this the way God wants us to live?" My response is no. The Lord told the Israelites to remember the Sabbath and to keep it holy. The Sabbath served as a holy day and a day of rest for both people and animals, commemorating God's rest after the work of creation.

The acceptable behavior for the Sabbath Day was set by God Himself. He set the example for His people to follow. He established the pattern. He determined and assigned value to the Sabbath. It was a day not to be used for common purposes. Remember, God abstained from working not because of any physical need but because everything was completed and nothing else was needed. However, for us physical rest was factored into the Sabbath equation.

Rest is a commodity that's so foreign to us today. I remember working all kinds of shifts and sometimes seven days a week. I worked overtime and on holidays. There was a period of time when I worked six days per week in addition to a part-time job, all the while attending state college as a full-time student. I subsisted on four hours of sleep per night. I don't believe I was alone in that insanity. There are people who work sixty to eighty hours a week and still spend their time off emailing, texting, and tweeting on social media. As believers, we spend so much time working, taking the kids to sports practice, and attending church functions that we have little or no time for real rest, worship, study, and being in God's presence.

But when we stop, pull back, and study the life of our Lord Jesus Christ, we will see that He set the standard for the Sabbath for all time. The Lord Jesus rested. He went to the cross to complete the work of redemption. He rested in that borrowed tomb on the Sabbath. He rose from the tomb early on the first day of the week. And He is now our Sabbath rest (see Hebrews chapters 3 and 4)—our ultimate Sabbath rest where, in the words of Job, "The wicked cease from troubling and there the weary are at rest" (Job 3:17).

The statute for the Sabbath comes through the Law, specifically out of the Ten Commandments:

> "Remember the Sabbath Day, to keep it holy. Six days you shall labor and do all your work, but the seventh day is the Sabbath of the Lord your God. In it you shall do no work: you, nor or your son, nor your daughter, nor your male, nor your female servant, nor your cattle, nor your stranger who is within your gates. For in six days the Lord made the heavens and the earth, the sea, and all that is in them, and rested on the seventh day. Therefore, the Lord blessed the Sabbath day and hallowed it. (Ex. 20:8–11 NKJV)

The command to remember was connected to Israel's future at a time when they were to enter and live in the Promised Land. God said about the Sabbath year, "You shall sow your land for six years and gather in its yield, but on the seventh year you shall let it rest and lie fallow, so that the needy of your people may eat; and whatever they leave the beast of the field may eat. You are to do the same with your vineyard and your olive grove." He went on to say about the Sabbath day, "Six days you are to do your work, but on the seventh day you shall cease from labor so that your ox and your donkey may rest, and the son of your female slave, as well as your stranger, may refresh themselves" (Ex. 23:10–12 NASB).

As a covenant people, Israel was to stop their weekly and everyday activities and honor God by resting and worshiping on the seventh day. It boiled down to a matter of obedience, faith, and trust. I don't know about you, but life under God's governing system seems so much better than what we have today. I don't think homelessness and hunger was an issue of concern for the people of Israel. (See also Ex. 16:27–30; 31:12–17.)

There is but one covenant between God and men. God, through the one covenant, in sovereign fashion, dispenses His grace to humans and fulfills His promises to them.

However, within the realm of the one covenant we find what I call codicil covenants or special circumstances covenants. For instance, look at God's covenant with Noah. In Genesis 9, verses 9–17, God initiates a covenant with Noah that was universal in scope. It was unconditional and everlasting. God made a promise to never destroy the world and sin by waters of a flood. The sign of the covenant was the rainbow. Then there is God's covenant with Abraham, found in chapter 15 of Genesis. God promised Abraham a land in which to live and descendants that would be too numerous to count. In his spiritual relationship with the Lord, Abraham believed and trusted God. He enjoyed God's blessings and fellowship. Circumcision was the sign of this covenant.

In Exodus chapter 24, we find God's covenant with the nation of Israel. At mount Sinai (Horeb) Israel was called to obey, trust, and worship God in gratitude for His provisions, recognizing all that they had come from Him. In 2 Samuel chapter 7, God gave a promise to King David. More information about this covenant is contained in Psalms 89 and 132 and Isaiah 55. The covenant stipulated that David's descendants would be known as God's sons and that his kingdom would be an everlasting kingdom.

This leads us to the final and lasting covenant, the "New Covenant." The Old Testament is full references of the new covenant—specifically found in the prophesies of Isaiah, Jeremiah, Ezekiel, and Hosea.

The significance of the Sabbath is that it was not only a day of rest for the nation of Israel but also a sign of God's covenant with them. The Sabbath was God consecrating and setting the children of Israel apart for sacred and kingdom purposes. Observing the day as God intended was a sign of obedience, faith, and trust in Him. In contrast to the rest of the world, which feverishly worked days upon days, Israel rested and took refuge in God on this special day. The Sabbath for Israel was a type of rest all believers have in Christ Jesus.

We know that our Sabbath rest is embodied in Jesus Christ our Lord. The Lord Jesus came to this earth to secure our redemption and restoration to a right relationship with God our Creator. His work, according to Matthew 18:11 and Luke 19:10, was to save that which was lost. When Jesus performed miraculous healings on the Sabbath, the Jews objected to his breaking the Law. After a lengthy dialogue, Jesus declared that His Father had been working until now and that He was presently working (Jo. 5:17). Then, in John 9:4,

Jesus said, "We must work the works of Him who sent Me as long as it is day; night is coming when no one can work" (NASB). All through the gospels we see the miraculous works of our Lord.

Night came when He went to the cross to complete the work of redemption. He rested in a borrowed tomb on God's Sabbath. He rose from the tomb on the first day of the week to become the ultimate Sabbath rest. His completed work eliminated the need for people to try to achieve salvation and eternal life by human effort. There was no more working, trying to get right with God. Christ became our righteousness. There was no need to try to gain God's approval and acceptance. We are accepted in the beloved. There was no need to continue labor under the heavy load of sin, shame, and guilt. The Lord Jesus invited us to come to Him, and He gives rest. By faith, through grace, we who believe and turn to God are saved, given eternal life, and enter into His rest.

CHAPTER 15: FOR THE REST OF THE STORY!

"This is the account of the heavens and the earth when they were created, in the day the Lord God made earth and heaven. Now no shrub of the field was yet in the earth, and no plant of the field had yet sprouted, for the Lord God had not sent rain upon the earth, and there was no man to cultivate the ground. But a mist used to rise from the earth and water the whole surface of the ground. Then the Lord God formed man of the dust of the ground and breathed into his nostrils the breath of life; and man became a living being."

—Genesis 2:4–7 NASB

A WORD ABOUT THE FIRST TWO chapters here in Genesis is needed at this point. Chapter 1 speaks to us about what God did in terms of setting time in motion and ordering the cosmos into being. And chapter 2 tells us how God did it. We call this a recapitulation—meaning, it is a dance between form and function. There is no discrepancy or conflict between the two chapters.

Chapter 2 gives some details as to how God did what He did in chapter 1 with creation. In chapter 1, we saw formation of the heavens, earth, waters (firmament above, and the oceans, seas, lakes, and rivers below), land, trees, shrubbery, heavenly bodies, animal life, and human life. Here in chapter 2, we see function. The earth would be rained upon as God enacted the water cycle and evaporation process. Trees, plants, grasses, and grains would appear because of the rain. Man, God's crown of creation—made in His image and likeness and the responsible steward of all that God created—comes to the forefront. The formatted dust and clay are the house, and the breath of God is life, God's image and likeness.

Paradise

> The Lord God planted a garden toward the east, in Eden; and there he placed the man whom he had formed. Out of the ground the Lord God caused to grow every tree that is pleasing to the sight and good for food; the tree of life also in the midst of the garden, and the tree of the knowledge of good and evil. Now a river flowed out of Eden to water the garden; and from there divided and became four rivers. The name of the first is Pishon; It flows around the whole land of Havilah, where there is gold. The gold of that land is good; the bdellium and onyx stone are there. The name of the second river is Gihon; It flows around the whole land of Cush. The name of the third river is Tigris; It flows east of Assyria. And the fourth river is the Euphrates. (Gen. 2:8–14 NASB)

The book of Revelation tells us all we need to know about paradise. We notice that there is one significant difference between paradise in Genesis and paradise in Revelation. Paradise in Revelation is void of the Tree of the Knowledge of Good and Evil.

I like how The Message Bible paraphrases the apostle John's account of paradise:

> Then the Angel showed me Water-of-Life River, crystal bright. It flowed from the Throne of God and the Lamb, right down the middle of the street. The Tree of Life was planted on each side of the River, producing twelve kinds of fruit, a ripe fruit each month. The leaves of the Tree are for the healing of the nations. Never again will anything be cursed. The Throne of God and of the Lamb is at the center. His servants will offer God service—worshiping, they'll look on his face, their foreheads mirroring God. Never again will there be any night. No one will need lamplight or sunlight. The shining of God, the Master, is all the light anyone needs. And they will rule with him age after age after age. (Rev. 22:1–5)

The apostle John is letting us know that sin and evil is done away with, and only righteousness and life is left standing.

A Gated Community

"Then the Lord God took the man and put him into the garden of Eden to cultivate it and keep it. … Out of the ground the Lord God formed every beast of the field and every bird of the sky and brought them to the man to see what he would call them; and whatever the man called a living creature, that was its name. The man gave names to all the cattle, and to the birds of the sky, and to every beast of the field" (Gen. 2:15, 19–20 NASB).

Pastor Dave Branon says that God created the world and the earth and placed it in our care. The problem is that we share this planet with so many others, we run the risk of seeing its beauty diminished and its resources depleted. Some, on an individual basis, put forth great efforts to preserve our planet and must see their efforts as valuable. But we need all to work together to do our part. Branon suggests we buy and consume less, simplify things, repair instead of replacing, reuse, and recycle as good stewards of God's good earth. I believe many people, companies, and organizations are trying to do a better job of separating compostable items from land fill or recyclable items, but we have a long way to go.

A friend of mine told me about the time he had a chance to joke with a man on his flight to the East Coast. He and the gentleman struck up a conversation about where they lived and the kind of work, they both did. The man said to my friend that he worked for a large corporation in Silicon Valley in the San Francisco Bay Area and lived in a gated community across the Bay in an area called Black Hawk. The gentleman turned to my friend and asked, "What about you?" My friend replied, "I formerly worked for a large corporation and lived in a gated community in Marin County, California." Truth is, he was formerly incarcerated in San Quentin State Prison for twenty-seven years and had worked in the laundry department. San Quentin was his gated community and working in its laundry department had been his job. I don't think the businessman had a clue of what type of gated community or employment situation my friend alluded to.

Adam and Eve lived in a better gated community than the corporate executive and had a much-higher-paying job. Their housing and employment were millions of times better than that of my friend. Here was both permanent housing and employment. I can only imagine that there are thousands of people wishing they had permanent employment and housing. I know one young lady who's only living situation is provided when house-sitting for family and friends while working a temporary job. She is trying to earn enough money to get her own place. She's also looking for permanent work. It was not that way with Adam and Eve. They had it made. The Eden community was a special place located in the middle of a perfect environment. It was a place of communion, worship, and fellowship. It was the "sanctuary" of God.

Work is important. We were created for both natural and spiritual work. As a matter of fact, the apostle Paul said if a man does not work, he should not eat (2 Thess. 3:10). Now, I know that this statement needs to be tempered a bit to address the appropriate situation, but work is important, and we are built for work. Work is a gift from God. Henry M. Morris said that it is a God-given privilege to be able to do useful work, whether that work consists of preaching God's Word or improving God's world.

We are not defined by our work; rather, contrary to the world's standard, we are defined by our worship. I'm not talking about weekly church meetings or worship services. Worship of God is much more than that. Worship is not just a song or two. Worship is not my white suit on First Sunday or the sisters with their "crowns" dressed in white. Worship is my daily living in the presence of God, my obedience and sacrifice to Him, and my unbroken fellowship with the Lord.

Yes, work is important, but it was not Adam's work or lack thereof that got him in trouble. It wasn't his slackness with work that bought for him a troubled lifestyle. It was his worship. He and Eve replaced their love for God, their homage to Him, with love of themselves. They and everybody born after them were thus tethered to sin and paid homage to "self" instead of God.

The garden—that gated community or sanctuary—was set up for Adam and Eve to both work for and worship their Creator. It was a place where they could fellowship and commune with Him as often as they desired. They had unfettered access to the Almighty, all-powerful Creator and lover of our souls.

The Power of Choice

"The Lord God made all sorts of trees grow up from the ground—trees that were beautiful and that produced delicious fruit. In the middle of the garden he placed the tree of life and the tree of the knowledge of good and evil. ... But the Lord God warned him, 'You may freely eat the fruit of every tree in the garden— except the tree of the knowledge of good and evil. It you eat its fruit, you are sure to die'" (Gen. 2:9, 16–17 NLT).

Did you know that there were two trees in the middle of the garden? One was the Tree of Life and the other the Tree of the Knowledge of Good and Evil. One tree led to a great life, while the other tree led to a gory life. One tree led to eternal life and the other tree led to death. And it's so strange to me that, over my lifetime, I've heard so much more about the Tree of the Knowledge of Good and Evil than I ever did about the Tree of Life. Why is that? What is it about us that we focus more on the "fallen" side of things rather than on the righteous side of things? I hear people in church and especially in the pulpit and choir section speak more of the Devil than they do of Jesus. Why is that? Maybe it's the residue of sin in us that we default to it so often.

Puzzling to me is that Adam and Eve had not experienced the reality of sin at that point. So, theirs was not a default to sin but to a more powerful reality. Theirs was a desire to delve into the mystery of God. By their own choosing, they decided to push the envelope. It was a bad move, as we shall see later on.

I wonder, though, what was so attractive and enticing about the Tree of the Knowledge of Good and Evil? Was it really the salesmanship of the enemy of life, or was its Eve's curiosity and craving for something she thought she might have been missing out on? Maybe it was a combination of the two.

When I read about the Tree of the Knowledge of Good and Evil in Genesis 2:9 and 17, I became curious as to what kind of fruit might the forbidden tree contain. I came up with what I believe describes the fruit (works) that sin went on to produce. This list is not exhaustive, nor is it something we should spend precious time debating. This is a list of human behavior and activities that people engaged in as noted in the Bible following Genesis chapter 3 and all the way through to the end of Revelation.

Fruit from the Forbidden Tree

Rejection of the Living God in favor of self or other gods	Disrespect/misuse of God's name	Idolatry	Dishonoring the Sabbath
Dishonoring/disrespect of father and mother	Murder	Adultery	Sexual immorality
Impure thoughts	Theft/stealing	False witnessing	Covetousness
Pride	Envy	Jealousy	Gluttony
Lust/lustful pleasure	Wild parties	Drunkenness	Greed
Sloth	Hostility	Anger/outburst of anger	Quarreling
Divisiveness	Selfish ambition	Everyone considered wrong except those in one's own group	Participation in demonic activity

Think about it: what an awesome opportunity! Here it is, right in front of them and staring them right in the face. Here was God's intention for them and everyone born to them. God intended that they were to have authority and power to rule over His earth. Adam and Eve were given the privilege and power to procreate—a privilege not afforded the angels. They were blessed with unlimited provisions. Their housing was situated in a prime location. They were given permanent employment. They were given the power of choice with only one prohibition.

This brings me to the "What if?" question. I taught a lesson once entitled "Choices and the Choices We Make." I focused on how a single choice could change the course or trajectory of a person's life. I've had some "what if?" moments. What about you? What if I had gone right instead of left? What if I had gotten out of there instead of staying? What if I had run out of there like Joseph ran from Potiphar's wife? Keep in mind that I'm not talking about "hindsight" wisdom, or second guessing, or having regrets. It's about where a different choice might have taken me in my journey.

In my spare time in the military, I was part of a singing group. We sang in clubs along the East Coast and in Canada. We actually cut a record, though it didn't sell many copies. But here in this "what if?" moment, I wondered what might have been if I had pursued a career in the entertainment field. How far could I have gone? What would my life look like now? Would I be living in California or some other part of the country or world? Would I have the same family or a different one? I wonder if Adam and Eve had "what if?" moments after having been expelled from the garden of Eden.

I once had a client I had been counseling whom I will call Bonnie. She put her academic pursuits and career goals on hold because she made the choice to become romantically involved with a guy. They stayed together for a period of time, but he moved out and on to someone else. He left Bonnie with a child to raise by herself. I can imagine there are hundreds or thousands of stories like Bonnie's. For fifteen years Bonnie poured herself into raising her daughter. She came to me because she and her daughter had some issues they needed to work through. After a series of meetings, Bonnie and her daughter made progress and reached resolution. However, Bonnie continued to meet with me to discuss some of her intermediate and long-term goals. In one of the sessions she shared her plans to go back to school and get a degree. She was looking to catch up on the dream she had prior to getting pregnant with her daughter.

While discussing her plans, the "what if?" question popped up. We talked about what her life might have looked like had she pursued college right after high school and established herself in a career. It was in that moment when feelings of frustration with her present condition surfaced. She had regrets—not about having given birth to her daughter but about the choices she made prior to getting pregnant with her daughter. Bonnie was like so many who look back and wished they had known better, believing they would have made better choices. However, the good part is that Bonnie decided to make her future overcome any regrets she had had with her past.

The possibility of eternal life was right at Adam and Eve's fingertips. And, last but not least, they had a right relationship with God, their Creator. The life of God was resident in their souls. What if they had chosen the Tree of Life instead of the Tree of the Knowledge of Good and Evil? I can only wonder what life today would have been like had Adam and Eve not disobeyed and rebelled against God.

Here is another thought. If sin had not entered the world through Adam and Eve, then through whom and how long would it have taken for sin to enter? Through what generation might sin have entered? Would sin have entered the world at all? Perhaps life would have continued to look like life in the first two chapters of Genesis had sin not entered into the world through the first couple. Can anyone imagine never being unemployed, sick, terminally ill, hungry, or afraid of dying? Would there have been death at all? Can you imagine a world without wars, a world without family or community conflict, or a world without crime and violence?

Here's a word to my good friends who think life would be boring if conflict did not exist. I don't need chaos to make life interesting. I would not be bored at all. There's too much about human life, animal life, and nature life to discover and appreciate for me to ever think I would be bored with a peaceful lifestyle. After all, if trouble, tribulation, chaos, and conflict was all that, then why are there so many people praying and fighting for peace? Why are we spending so much of our time and effort trying to reach peace accords? Why aren't we celebrating chaos, drama, and conflict? Why don't we have a chaos, drama, and conflict holiday?

How can one ever be bored when there is so much to discover about the mysteries of our magnificent, all-knowing, all-powerful, and ever-present God? There is so much about God that we have yet to discover. Solomon said, "He has made everything appropriate in its time. He has also set eternity in their heart, yet so that man will not find out the work which God has done from the beginning even to the end." (Eccl. 3:11 NASB). It may or may not be the case where we will know so much about God in the world to come.

I personally know a lot of people whose lives are dominated by boredom. Instead of living thriving lives, theirs is a life of survival. A lot of us live from paycheck to paycheck with little or no savings, but my bored acquaintances may be worse off. They go deeper into debt to take vacations, and while they are on vacation, they "pinch" pennies just to keep up appearances. At home, they commute for long hours to jobs for which they are grateful but secretly wish they had a job that was more rewarding.

Boredom is young people choosing the criminal lifestyle on the false promise of wealth, fine cars, and the girl or guy. Money, power, and fame is all yours! You can have it! It's all exciting at first, it's the dream, but it soon turns into a nightmare. Their lifestyle becomes an ugly journey down a dark road going nowhere. Many of them go from the streets to prison, from prison to parole, from parole violation to the county jails, and from the county jails to probation, and back to the streets and perhaps homeless. It makes me think of the 1969 song by The Friends of Distinction called "Going in Circles." One of the lines of the song says, "You got me going in circles, (oh round and round I go) …" Did God intend for their lives to be like that? Absolutely not!

With the placement of both trees there in the middle of the garden with only one restriction, God gave Adam and Eve the power to choose. God never coerces or forces anyone to choose Him. Rather, He is glorified when people of their own free will make Him their choice. Better stated, we say "yes" to Him because He's said "yes" to us. We love Him because He first loved us (1 Jo. 4:19).

Life in the garden had all been prepared for man's habitation and God's visitation. It was a perfect environment for perfect human beings. Adam and Eve had not sinned at this point. The earth was a world filled with great possibilities. God was pleased, and man was at ease.

What more did they need? It just doesn't get any better than that. God's plans are sure, and they bring success, joy, and prosperity.

CHAPTER 16: THE NEED FOR A HELPER!

Then the Lord God said, 'It is not good for the man to be alone; I will make him a helper suitable for him.'... But for Adam there was not found a helper suitable for him."

—*Gen. 2:18, 20*

MARVIN WILLIAMS TELLS THE STORY about California's state prison system comprising thirty-three different facilities where twenty-five thousands of the world's most dangerous inmates endure solitary confinement in small concrete cells. He says, "They have virtually no contact with the outside world." And in Oregon's state penitentiary, an inmate said that the most difficult part about isolation is not being able to see somebody face-to-face—to communicate, to touch, to hug, to feel loved, or feel human. Their words scream: "We are lonely!"

This is not the way things are supposed to be. Whether deserved or not, loneliness is a devastating proposition. God created us to be in close relationships with others (Eccl. 4:9–12) and with Him (Rev. 21:3). He showed in creating Eve that people were meant to enjoy companionship, love, intimacy, and romance, and someone with whom they could communicate and share of themselves.

God said that it was not good for the man to be alone. I have found over the years that many have taken the word *alone* to mean that Adam was lonely. I choose a different perspective about whether Adam was lonely or not. I believe that one can be alone and not be lonely. And, likewise, one can be lonely in the company of lots of people. There are lonely people who attend church gatherings every week while surrounded by lots of fellow worshippers but who still feel the sting of loneliness. In Bible College, I was taught to interpret single verses of Scripture within their context or grouping of their subject matter. That meant that if I looked at Adam as being alone, it is within the context of God placing him in the garden and giving him the responsibility to "cultivate" it and "keep" it (Gen. 2: 15–25). At the same time, Adam needed to fulfill the mandate (Gen. 1:28), which was to have children and populate the earth. Obviously, Adam would have to have some help with keeping God's commands.

Just because God said that is was not good for Adam to be alone did not necessarily mean that Adam was lonely. Most people who read or write about these verses tend to conclude that Adam's condition was one of loneliness and in need of a companion and sexual partner. To a certain degree this is true, but I don't believe it was the primary consideration.

Spiros Zodhiates, general editor of the Hebrew-Greek Key Study Bible, says, "Man immediately set about to explore and define his domain. God wanted him to come to the conclusion that he was different from all the animals, that bestiality was wrong. He needed a matching sexual partner which corresponded to his own nature."

This view is also reflected in an article in the Standard Lesson Commentary entitled "God Plans a Help Meet for Man" (1993–1994):

> No creature like Adam existed in all the animal kingdom. He was alone, and God saw that that was not good. Animals make great pets and frequently provide a measure of companionship for lonely people. They also are helpful as beasts of burdens. But not one of them has the spiritual, intellectual, emotional, or moral capacity of a human being. God saw that man needed the companionship of a being like himself and so He set out to make a mate for the man He created. The two would stand side by side. They would complement each other, aid each other, and in every way be suitable for each other.

I don't believe Adam could have handled his caretaking duties all by himself. I believe it was necessary for him to have someone like himself, a reasoning rational human being, to help him. He certainly could not procreate by himself. He needed a helper divinely designed with the capacity to carry and give birth to children. Remember, God ordered the population of His earth in chapter 1 of Genesis. The other important feature to consider is that every set of species (animals and plants) was ordered to reproduce after their own kind. It goes without saying that a human-animal coupling would not work for God's purposes.

Adam needed a helper! More than that, he needed a suitable helper. Domesticated animals could have been of some help to the man, but they didn't seem suitable for what God had in mind for Adam and his responsibilities. A note on Genesis 2:20—the New Revised Standard Version Bible records, "to be fully human one needs to be in relation to others who correspond to oneself. Helper, not in a relationship of subordination but of mutuality and interdependence."

The context for verse 20 speaks of responsibility and more specifically Adam and Eve's caretaking duties as assigned by God. King Solomon said, "Two people are better off than one, for they can help each other succeed. If one person falls, the other can reach out and help" (Eccl. 4:9–10 NLT). Mark records that Jesus sent his disciples out in pairs to declare the "good news" and minister to the needs of the people of Israel. I believe the plan all along was to have two distinct and unique individuals—each possessing gifts, skills, talents, abilities, and qualities—come together for the purpose of exercising stewardship duties over God's earth.

The other point to be made here is that Eve was not an afterthought as some might suggest. Eve was in God's plan from eternity. God, in His infinite wisdom, knew already what Adam would need. Someone suggested that God created the male, brought the animals forth to be identified and named, and then created Eve. We have no insight into what Adam might have been thinking at the time. Moses, the writer of Genesis, doesn't give us any details about it. A considerable amount of time might have passed between creating Adam and the making of Eve. How long of a time that period might have been, we don't know? Suffice it to say that Adam had time to observe and consider his caretaking responsibilities. Now, how he may have reacted to his conclusions about what he had to do, we don't know except that Scripture says that God saw or observed something about Adam and the challenge before him. The important thing is God wanted a suitable helper for Adam. However, the creation of Eve didn't seem to happen right away.

The Standard Lesson Commentary states that one may wonder why there was a delay in the creation of the woman, since God knew that she was necessary part of the picture. Several suggestions come to mind. One is that her separate creation emphasized her importance. Another is that she was created only after the man recognized his need for her. Nothing in the animal parade over which Adam officiated came close to filling the bill. The fact that God had said that it was not good for the man to be alone signified how vital this final creative act really was. The woman was just the helper and companion the man needed—and still needs.

A Special Surgery!

"So, the Lord God caused Adam to fall into a deep sleep. While the man slept, the Lord God took out one of the man's ribs and closed up the opening. Then the Lord God made a woman from the rib, and he brought her to the man. 'At Last,' the man exclaimed, 'This one is bone from my bone, and flesh from my flesh! She will be called 'woman,' because she was taken out of a 'man.'" (Gen. 2:21–23 NLT).

The Bible was not written to be a science book, but you can see all the disciplines of science in it. I am continually amazed at the position people from the various religious traditions and cultures take toward medicine—medical personnel in general and doctors and surgeons in particular. I'm not one to divide life into two camps with faith on one side and science on the other. Let me be clear. It doesn't matter at this point whether medical personnel or doctors believe in God or not. It doesn't matter whether they believe they've been given a special ability to learn what they've learned, know what they know, and do what they can do. I believe we all come to the table with a script and certain gifts, talents, and skills.

We have the choice of believing we are humble gifted servants of God or self-made individuals. I believe we are made in God's image and likeness to function as His representatives on earth. I believe that God embedded in us the ability to study plant life, animal life, and human life to develop ways to sustain life through medical means. God made medicine possible when He provided the plants, herbs, elements, and substances of the earth. People who study and practice medicine are blessed by God to learn what they learned and do what they do. It's not God's fault that sinful man takes what God meant for good and turns it into an evil enterprise. Humans, with their power of choice, are the ones who take what God created for good and use it to abuse, exploit, and oppress their fellow humans.

The great surgeon and healer put Adam to sleep and with His divine scalpel cut through skin and tissue to reach his rib cage. Then, with His divine saw, He cut out part of Adam's rib. From that rib, the Creator of life fashioned Eve. Having completed Eve, God presented her to Adam.

God is amazing, He loves to give His children gifts. Christmas and birthdays were always special for me because I love to give my children gifts and watch their faces light up. In giving Adam his wife, Eve, God presented His son with the gift of a bride. God did the same for His Son Jesus in making the church a bride for Christ. Ephesians tells us that Christ's bride, the church, will be presented in all her glory, without spot or blemish (Eph. 5:22–23).

Adam recognized that his Eve was of his own flesh and bone. She was someone equal to him—intelligent, beautiful, and capable of helping him with his God-given responsibilities.

Adam's reaction at the sight of Eve was very interesting. "This is now bone of my bones and flesh of my flesh; she shall be called Woman, because she was taken out of man," Adam said. He looked at Eve and seemed to have been mesmerized by what he saw. Adam was impressed with the wife God had designed for their marriage.

Adam's words and expressions seemed to be a sign of his gratitude for the gift God had given him. But in chapter 3 of Genesis, all that seemed to change. Eve was deceived by the serpent, and Adam, in my estimation, failed to protect her. They disobeyed God, ate from the forbidden tree, and were instantly introduced to some emotionally troubling realities. The two, for the first time, experienced shame, guilt, fear, and anger.

Remember Adam's reaction when God first presented her to him? Remember, it was bone of my bones, flesh of my flesh? What had been "bone of my bones" suddenly became "… the woman you gave me." (Gen. 2:23; 3:12). Here is a common behavior that's so typical of all of us. We fail to take responsibility for our actions. Was Adam blaming God as well as Eve for predicament he found himself locked into? As I read this account, it seems to me that there may have been some angry overtones to Adam's response. I heard a story about a husband and wife who went to their church pastor for couple counseling. The husband walked in with pages and pages of paper representing complaints he had against his wife. After hours and hours of uninterrupted discourse from the husband, the pastor could no longer constrain himself.

"Brother," the pastor said, "if your wife is as you say she is, why did you marry her?"

Right away the husband shot back. He said, "Pastor, she wasn't like this at the beginning. She was not at all like she is now."

The pastor replied, "So, then, what you are telling me is that your wife only got this way after having been married to *you* all these years." Adam, like this husband, was placing all the blame for their predicament on his wife, Eve. He, like this husband, was taking no responsibility for having played his part in the problem.

Another problem I hear today is the statement "It's not your fault." This statement is used quite a lot on TV and in the movies. I believe that in a feeble effort to be supportive of people, we actually discourage them from taking responsibility for their actions. Sometimes it's not the person's fault. But, at other times, somebody has to take responsibility and own up to the problem.

Marriage God's Style!

"This explains why a man leaves his father and mother and is joined to his wife, and the two are united into one. Now the man and his wife were both naked, but they felt no shame" Gen. 2:24–25 NLT).

The Bible teaches us that marriage is a divine institution, ordained and regulated by God's Word. One year my wife and I attended an annual couples' conference sponsored by our local church. The main speaker was making a point that it was the man's job to go on a responsible search for his wife. His point was that it was better for a bride to wait on God to bring the right person to her rather than for her to go looking for "Mr. Right." I took it that his point was based on the part of the Scripture that read "a man leaves his father and mother and is joined to his wife ..." As a matter of fact, his three main points were the man leaves, he cleaves, and they become one. Since that time, I've often wondered if the concept of God making, knowing, and choosing Eve, then bringing her and presenting her to Adam worked much better than the way people get together in today's time. I say this because only God really knows what He wants out the marriage of the two people. Would a God-arranged marriage like the one Adam and Eve had work out better even with its good and bad times, ups and downs, conflicts and casualties? Would a God-arranged marriage, one totally offered back to God as a living sacrifice, reduce the number of divorces in society and the church? I don't know; I just wonder.

I am fully aware that things are different in different communities of people, cultures, and societies. So, I'm not here to impose some general rule on any person or group. People are free to choose whatever they want. They are free to decide the course and lifestyle by which they will live. That freedom of choice comes directly from God himself and not some legislative body.

People are asking whether marriage works for them. A 2012 study about societal attitudes toward marriage found that half of those surveyed said that society is just as well off when people have other priorities. In other words, 60% of the people surveyed ages 18–29 and 53% ages 30–49 believe society functions just fine with people pursuing pursuits other than marriage.

Marriage comes in many different forms. People are embracing the idea of serial monogamous marriages, in which they get married two or three times, seeking a different partner for each phase of their adult life. Then there are open marriages with their extramarital romps, in which passion, freedom, and self-expression are more important than physical exclusivity. There are commuter marriages in which couples still married live in separate cities for career-related reasons. People are moving in and living together as a test for marriage at a later time. Still others just get together and wait to see where it all goes.

There are also same-sex marriages that have become the rallying cry of many in the political realm. Priscilla Yamin says, "The question of same-sex marriage rights is about the inclusion of gays and lesbians not only concerning their private rights of citizens to marry but also their public rights of belonging. The freedom to marry is a fundamental right that should not have to be won or defended at the ballot box."

People have a right to choose, but it is up to God to judge and conclude. Love your neighbor, people, love your neighbor! And, finally, there are the traditional couplings that we called in the old days "shacking up" as well as "common law" relationships in which people say they are committed to each other and living together but really don't need any papers to tell them whether they are married or not.

Regardless of the position anyone might take on the issue of marriage, I believe God instituted marriage, ordained, and blessed the relationship for His own purpose. Adam and Eve's relationship was a God-arranged, God-ordained covenant relationship that included God in the equation. Adam and Eve had everything they would ever need. Henry Morris says they were one "flesh," each complementing the nature of the other, physically, mentally, and spiritually. He notes that before the entrance of sin into this family, the Scripture describes them as being naked and not ashamed. Adam and Eve's physiological makeup was complementary and divinely created in accordance with God's purpose and plan for their lives. They had an up-close and personal relationship with the Creator.

Permit me to raise a caution flag here. I don't believe marriage was for everyone born. I used to teach classes on spiritual gifts, and one of the issues dealt with whether some people were gifted to be married while others were gifted to live single and celibate lives. Quite a few of my students had to wrestle with the issue of their families pressuring them to get married and have children. These students believed they were born to live single, celibate lives and had aspirations of serving on the mission field. Sometimes the pressure to be married came from family members. Other times, the pressure came from close friends. Still, at other times, the pressure to marry came from fellow members and leaders in their church group. From wherever the pressure came, it had a powerfully negative effect on my counselees.

I like how the apostle Paul dealt with the issue in 1 Corinthians chapter 7. He spoke of how there is a difference of gifting between people. There are those gifted to live single, celibate lives who are able to offer God undivided, loyal service. Those individuals are able to devote their time, talents, and resources strictly to serving God by ministering to the needs of other people. But, for the married people, Paul says that their time, talents, and resources are going to be divided between God and their families. There is absolutely nothing wrong with either path in life. They are both under the watch and care of the Father, God. His will is to be done on earth as it is done in heaven. His purpose is to be served whether a person is married or single.

I raise this issue here because I believe that the concept of being a "helper" goes beyond our relationship status. I believe that in the grand scheme of things we are all helpers of one another in this great family of God and, in the words of the older folk, whether married, single, male, female, young, old, rich, or poor.

CHAPTER 17: PATHOS IN PARADISE

PATHOS IS A WORD MEANING an experience in life or a work that stirs up emotions of pity, sympathy, and sorrow. Pathos comes from an ancient Greek word meaning "suffering."

God clearly intended that the heavens, the earth, the animals, and the people He created function in ways that bring glory and honor to His name.

At the end of Genesis chapter 1, the Bible describes the condition of God's creative work as being "very good." But creation didn't stay that way. Something happened! Something very catastrophic happened. Our first parents picked a good day to make a bad decision. What happened? Unfortunately for them, they chose to go against their God, the true and living God.

The Day the World Changed

We know that it was not any fault on God's part that things did not work out the way He intended them to. Adam and Eve used their power and authority to choose to make the decision they made. Theirs was a decision that negatively impacted all humankind, including nature life and animal life for generations to come.

Scripture cautions us to seek counsel before making major life decisions. The Bible says, "Without consultation, plans are frustrated, but with many counselors they succeed" (Prov. 15:22 NASB).

I often wondered why Eve seemed to not have taken a step back and consulted with the Lord about her conversation with the serpent. Did she or didn't she talk with Adam about what was going on? Certainly, God was near, and Scripture describes her husband as being with her. However, it does not tell us whether she got advice or directions from either source.

Now, I'm not one to place all the blame on Eve. There is something to be said about her husband, Adam, if he had been around when the conversation was taking place between the serpent and his wife. Scripture tell us that "her husband who was with her …" Was he there all along? Or was he just there when Eve decided to eat the forbidden fruit? At the same time, I wonder what was it that made Adam so powerless to protect his wife from that third-party intruder into their marriage.

There is nothing in the world that ruins a marriage more readily than a third-party intruder. This idea of a third-party intruder was one of the topics often discussed in our premarriage counseling meetings and seminars. In those meetings, we identified what I called "third-party intruders." In our discussions, we talked about how the identified intruders may impact the couple's marriage, as well as how to protect the relationship from said intruders for the long haul. We discussed how in-laws, single friends, or careers may serve as intruders if no limits or boundaries were set in place in the relationship.

There are other intruders—and I hate to cast them as such—that we must consider. We love them dearly. They are bundles of joy. But they require our utmost attention and time. It is a blessing and a privilege to have children. In fact, Adam and Eve's mandate from God was to be fruitful, multiply, and populate the earth with children. Unfortunately, when the little ones come along, many couple relationships take a huge hit in terms of intimacy and romance. For example, a wife may focus all her time and attention on the home and raising the kids while the husband pours himself into the job or career. Over time, they grow apart, and their intimacy and romance fall by the wayside. This is also true in the reverse. The father takes the stay-at-home position, and the wife is the breadwinner. Or both work outside the home and share childrearing responsibilities. In any case, over the years their schedules and interests are divided, and they find themselves total strangers once the kids are grown up and out of the house. The task of rebuilding intimacy and romance becomes a huge challenge for them. Though, this is not the case for all couples, because some find ways to strike a balance between work and parental responsibilities.

Adam and Eve did not have children or in-laws to deal with as third-party intruders, but there was a stranger who was allowed to invade their home and caused great harm to their marriage. So, what happened?

Adam and his wife found themselves in the midst of a perfect storm. All the elements that make up a conflicting moment was present. This was a storm that they had not faced before. They were not prepared for the onslaught of the enemy. They found themselves tossed "to and fro" by winds of deception. Their lives were flooded with waves of lies. And, worst of all, they failed to seek disaster relief.

In his book *The Battle for the Beginning*, John MacArthur says,

> Genesis 3 is one of the most vitally important chapters in all the Bible. It is the foundation of everything that comes after it. Without it, little else in Scripture or in life itself would make sense. … Genesis 3 explains the condition of the universe and the state of humanity. It explains why the world has so many problems. It explains the human dilemma. It explains why we need a Savior. And it explains what God is doing in history. When God completed His perfect creation, there was no disorder, no chaos, no conflict, no struggle, no pain, no discord, no deterioration, and no death. Yet our lives today are filled with all those things all the time. … Frankly, we find it hard to imagine what a perfect world would have been like. Genesis 3 explains how we got from that paradise of unimaginable perfection to where we are today. (2001, p. 195)

When God breathed into his nostrils, Adam's body was infused with the "Life of God." He was animated, and he became a living soul. William P. Barker said, "Adam was put on earth to live obediently and responsibly before God and given freedom to enjoy every part of creation except the tree of knowledge of good and evil." Adam's wife was named Eve because she was the mother of all living humans. Her name in

Hebrew means "life-giving." Barker says that Eve, like Adam, rebelled against God and put her own plans and wisdom ahead of God's. Her disobedience triggered Adam's and produced the chain reaction of anxiety and guilt in every person, and the estrangement between God, man and woman, brothers, nations, and races continues to this day.

An Intrusive Visitor

Now the serpent was more crafty than any beast of the field which the Lord God had made" (Gen 3:1 NASB).

After having painted such a beautiful picture of God's intent for life on earth, Moses starts chapter 3 of Genesis with the word *now*, as if to say that you've heard the good news, now let me give you the bad news. John MacArthur says:

> We are not to think God created reptiles with the ability to talk and reason. The cunning (craftiness) this particular serpent displayed is not a characteristic of serpents in general. What is described here is something more than a mere animal; he is a being who knew God, a personality who spoke with great intelligence and shrewdness. He was a being who was opposed to God. He was deceptive, hostile, and bent on destroying the moral innocence of the first couple. (2001, p. 195)

I believe he might have been very jealous of the kind of worship given to God. The way in which the angels and elders worshiped God must have made that overly ambitious bystander and observer to all that was taking place at the moment very envious. You know him. John says in Revelation 12:9 that he is the great dragon, serpent of old who is called the Devil and Satan, who deceives the whole world. Jesus, in Luke 10:18, says he saw Satan fall from heaven like lightning. Isaiah implies he was the one who was cut down to the earth, who had weakened the nations (Isa. 14:12 NASB). He was the anointed cherub. He sang together with the morning stars and shouted for joy with the angels.

There was no shortage of praise associated with this created being. He had a great following, the leader of a host of other angelic beings. But this was not enough for him. No, he was ambitious, wanting more—so much more and more than he could handle. He had a problem, and later he became a problem—for human beings, that is.

What was his problem, you ask? Scripture says wickedness was found in him. He was filled with violence, and his heart became proud because of his beauty, and his wisdom became corrupt. This being had the audacity to declare to his cronies that he was going to ascend the tops of the clouds and make himself like the high God. He boasted that he would ascend to heaven and raise his throne above the stars of God. Really! He had ideas of sitting enthroned on the mount of assembly, on the utmost heights of the sacred mountain. Are you kidding me, seriously? The created one was going to unseat the One who created him? What a joke. What we have here is a case of gross self-deception.

Ironically, deception was the strategy he used to trick Adam and Eve into going against God in the garden of Eden. It's the same strategy he employs against people today. He wants to replace God in our hearts with himself. "All these things I will give You, if you will fall down and worship me"

(Matt. 4:9 NKJV). These are the very words he spoke to Jesus, Son of the living God, in the wilderness. Oh, come on, man! Am I to believe the Devil was going to give Jesus something He already owns?

Of course, I understand that the Devil might have been speaking to the humanness in Jesus, but had Jesus lost sight of His divine self and sovereignty over all that exists? I choose to think not. He created everything, and everything exists by Him. John said in his gospel that all things came into being through Him and apart from Him nothing came into being that exists (Jo. 1:1–3). The Devil was after the faith and worship that belonged only to God, our Father.

Warning, a level-five alert! A reckoning was about to happen. The Most High had a death blow response for this rebellious creature. God said to the overly ambitious, jealous one that he would be brought down to the grave. People would stare at and mock him. God finally drove him from the mount of God in disgrace and expelled him from heaven along with a third of the angels who had aligned themselves with him. The lesson here is evil will never triumph over good, sin will never triumph over righteousness, no one will ever be able to defeat God, and nothing will ever defeat God's purpose.

This overly ambitious being of which I speak goes by several names and titles. He's called Lucifer, the serpent, the Devil, the enemy, and Satan (the accuser). Could it be that he had the nerve to accuse God of being unfair? If this really happened, it wouldn't be the only time he accused God of being unfair (see Isa. 14:13–23).

Remember the conversation he had with God concerning Job. Scripture says there was a day when the angels came to present themselves before the Lord. Satan must have still had access to the proceedings because he came there as well. God asked him from where he came. He replied, "From roaming throughout the earth, going back and forth on it" (Job 1:7 NIV).

God challenged him to test his strategy on Job. God described Job as honest, true to his word, totally devoted to God, and hating evil. But even here Satan played the unfair card. Satan said, in essence, "So you think Job does all that out of the sheer goodness of his heart? Why, no one ever had it so good! You pamper him like a newborn. You make sure nothing bad ever happens to him or his family or his possessions. You bless everything he does—he can't lose!" Then he added, "What do you think would happen if you reached down and took away everything that is his? He'd curse you right to your face, that's what would happen" (Job 1:8–12).

Ladies and gentlemen, you know the rest of the story. The key here is God was being accused of bribing Job, and that's the only reason Job was loyal to Him. Unfortunately, the same thing is happening today. Job was with God and for God. People today are with God as long as He is throwing out a few blessings here and there. The other part of the accusation from Satan was that God was being partial and unfair in his dealings with His created beings. Come on now—is God unfair? Does God show partiality? Absolutely not! We can trust Scripture, which tells us that there is no partiality with God (Rom. 2:11). There are no favorites when it comes to the Lord.

How might God have answered the Devil? He might have asked Satan to think back to the beginning. God might have had the Devil remember what He said about the One (the Redeemer), the seed of the woman, that was to come. He might have reminded Satan that the seed of the woman would crush his head and that he (Satan) would bruise the redeemer's heel (Gen. 3:15). Oh, by the way, Jesus was virgin born, to a low-income-producing tradesman in a less-than-ideal location on the globe. He grew up in a town that had a very bad reputation. On top of all that, He was made a little lower than the gods. So, you can see that, in doing so, God leveled the playing field. Jesus had nothing. He had no place to lay His head. He didn't have a ranch or large farm in which to live a comfortable life. He lived a nomadic lifestyle. As a matter of fact, at first, He was born into a family that saw Him as an embarrassment to them and urged Him to stop doing what He was sent to do. Yet, He never turned against the Father. He was persecuted, He suffered, went to the cross, died, and then went to the grave totally loyal, totally trusting, and committed to God. Silence, not another word was spoken! The enemy had no response to this heavenly truth.

At that point, God might have turned to Moses and said, "I want you to record all I am about to tell you. Write about the creation of the heavens and the earth and how I intended things to be. Existing in time, there will be nature life, animal life, and human life. First, I will create a physical world to house all the physical properties and physical beings. I will construct their world so that both humans and animals will have everything they need to live and lack nothing. There will be pleasure and enjoyment beyond their imagination. Nature life will be complete with its seasons and functioning according to divine order. The earth will be filled with animals and creatures each having an important role in the environment. And then there will be people created with the capacity to caretake, govern, and fill the earth with more people like themselves."

The Devil, my friends, is not to be played with or taken lightly. He is our enemy, and Jesus said that the enemy comes only to steal, kill, and destroy. Then the Lord Jesus declared that he came to give life (abundantly and eternal) to everyone who receives Him (Jo. 10:10).

The Bible doesn't tell us how Satan became evil. We don't know whether he was tempted in some way by some unknown source or not. All I know is that this is another one of those mysteries of God about which we will have to wait until the end to find out what happened. And for us, in our daily lives, it's not important how the enemy became what he is. The fact is that he is, and he exerts a lot of time and energy getting us to buy into and participate in his schemes.

I was asked the question one time by a dear lady if we should pray for the Devil and his fallen followers. I assumed at the time she meant if we should pray for the Devil to repent and ask God to forgive him. But I thought of a greater question: Would the Devil actually repent? Judas Iscariot was remorseful but didn't repent. He committed suicide.

In an article by Melinda Givin, I was reminded that the enemy's fate was sealed (Rev. 20:10). Givin said, "Pray for the remission of evil … but don't pray for evil's change of mind. If evil changes its mind, evil ceases to be. There is no evil-becoming-good, only decay and death ceasing to exist. At that point, all that is left is Being, which is uncorrupted goodness, and God." Here's a question: Should we sympathize or empathize with someone who is diametrically opposed to God, someone who after thousands of years still wants to unseat God and take His throne? And the Devil wants to accomplish that by deceiving and influencing people to embrace unrighteousness.

The enemy, by choice, has a bent toward evil, and Scripture has much to say about him. What, then, can we learn from Scripture about this crafty creature?

The prophet Isaiah prophesied against the king of Babylon, and as with the prophesy in Ezekiel against the king of Tyre, I believe the prophecy applies not just the earthly king but also to a supernatural source of evil. Isaiah says:

> "How you are fallen from heaven, O shining star, son of the morning! You have been thrown down to the earth, you who destroyed the nations of the world. For you said to yourself, 'I will ascend to heaven and set my throne above God's stars. I will preside on the mountain of the gods far away in the north. I will climb to the highest heavens and be like the Most High.' Instead, you will be brought down to the place of the dead, down to its lowest depths. Everyone there will stare at you and ask, 'Can this be the one who shook the earth and made the kingdoms of the world tremble? Is this the one who destroyed the world and made it into a wasteland? Is this the king who demolished the world's greatest cities and had no mercy on his prisoners?' The kings of the nations lie in stately glory, each in his own tomb. But you will be thrown out of your grave like a worthless branch. Like a corpse trampled underfoot, you will be dumped into a mass grave with those killed in battle. You will descend to the pit. You will not be given a proper burial, for you have destroyed your nation and slaughtered

> your people. The descendants of such an evil person will never again receive honor. Kill this man's children! Let them die because of their father's sins! They must not rise and conquer the earth, filling the world with their cities. This is what the Lord of Heaven's Armies says, "I, myself, have risen against Babylon! I will destroy its children and its children's children," says the Lord. "I will make Babylon a desolate place of owls, filled with swamps and marshes. I will sweep the land with the broom of destruction. I, the Lord of Heaven's Armies, have spoken!" (Isa. 14:12–23 NLT)

The prophet Ezekiel says that Lucifer was an anointed angelic guardian (28:14, 16). And that he had been cast from the mountain of God. As I said before, the Ezekiel passage was spoken against the king of Tyre, but, as John MacArthur puts it, it prophetically reached beyond the earthly king to the supernatural source of Satan's wickedness, pride, and corrupted authority.

> "Son of Man sing this funeral song for the king of Tyre. Give him this message from the Sovereign Lord: 'You were the model of perfection, full of wisdom and exquisite in beauty. You were in Eden, the garden of God. Your clothing was adorned with every precious stone—red carnelian, pale-green peridot, white moonstone, blue-green beryl, onyx, green jasper, blue lapis lazuli, turquoise, and emerald—all

> beautifully crafted for you and set in the finest gold. They were given to you on the day you were created. I ordained and anointed you as the mighty angelic guardian. You had access to the holy mountain of God and walked among the stones of fire. You were blameless in all you did from the day you were created until the day evil was found in you. Your rich commerce led you to violence, and you sinned. So, I banished you in disgrace from the mountain of God. I expelled you, O mighty guardian, from your place among the stones of fire. Your heart was filled with pride because of all your beauty. Your wisdom was corrupted by your love of splendor. So, I threw you to the ground and exposed you to the curious gaze of kings. You defiled your sanctuaries with your many sins and your dishonest trade. So, I brought fire out from within you, and it consumed you. I reduced you to ashes on the ground in the sight of all who were watching. All who knew you are appalled at your fate. You have come to a terrible end, and you will exist no more." (Ezek. 28:12–19 NLT)

The apostle John says that the intruder, who is the great dragon—the ancient serpent called the Devil, or Satan, the one deceiving the whole world—was thrown down to the earth with all his angels (Rev. 12:9).

I don't believe Eve had any idea of the power she was up against. We have knowledge of the enemy because we have Scripture. Eve did not have the Scriptures. Consider how shrewd and calculating the adversary is in his attempts to undermine our destiny in Christ Jesus. The enemy is skilled at influencing people toward evil.

Lately, we have become accustomed to influencers in social media. They are people who built a reputation for their knowledge and expertise on particular topics. They make regular posts about various topics on social media channels and generate large followings of enthusiastically engaged people who pay close attention to their views. As followers of Christ, we must not buy into the schemes of the enemy. It is imperative that we are fully aware of what's at stake when it comes to the Devil and his diabolical assault on our lives. We must be on guard. The apostle Peter tells us to be alert and vigilant when it comes to the enemy, who is like a roaring lion seeking to devour us (1 Pet. 5:8).

The enemy is a master influencer. An influencer is an individual who has the power to affect purchase decisions of others because of his authority, knowledge, position, or relationship with his audience. The Devil uses evil as a tool to try to exert his will in people's lives. He uses evil to slander God. He is successful in getting people to blame God for disasters, catastrophes, and chaos in the world. Is a tornado an act of God, or is it the result of cursed nature due to the sin of Adam and Eve? Is it not the result of converging weather patterns and conflicting wind currents? Bottom line: when you peel away all the layers, droughts, hurricanes, tornados, earthquakes, etc., are the result of the ground being cursed because of Adam. God did not curse Adam directly; He cursed the ground from which Adam's livelihood would come. In cursing the ground, God was putting a curse on all of nature life. God didn't cause Adam and Eve to sin—they chose to sin.

And by their choice, nature, in some ways, became dysfunctional and disorderly.

The fact is, the Devil initiated warfare against human beings. He uses his ability to deceive people and exercise influence over their life's choices. Satan wants God's crown of creation to perish in darkness with him and his band of fallen followers. Francis Frangipani says:

> When Satan rebelled against God, he was placed under eternal judgement in what the Bible calls "pits" or "bonds" of darkness. The devil, and the fallen angels with him, have been relegated to live in darkness. This darkness does not simply mean "lightless regions" or areas void of visible light. The eternal darkness to which this scripture (Jude 6) refers is essentially a moral darkness, which does ultimately degenerate to literal darkness. However, its cause is not simply the absence of light, it is the absence of God, who is Light. It is vital to recognize that this darkness to which Satan has been banished is not limited to areas outside of humanity. Unlike those who do not know Jesus, however, we have been delivered out of the domain or "authority" of darkness (Col. 1:13). We are not trapped in darkness if we have been born of light. But if we tolerate darkness through tolerance of sin, we leave ourselves vulnerable for satanic assault. For wherever there is willful disobedience to the Word of God, there is spiritual darkness and the potential for demonic activity.

"Satan," Francis says, "has a legal access, given to him by God, to dwell in the domain of darkness. We must grasp this point: The devil can traffic in any area of darkness, even the darkness that still exists in a Christian's heart." Knowing this about the enemy and all who reject God, it vitally important that we not take him lightly or underestimate his power to influence people to do his biddings.

A Deadly Dialogue

"He said to the woman, 'Has God indeed said, "You shall not eat of every tree of the garden?"' And the woman said to the serpent, "We may eat of the fruit of the trees in the garden; but of the fruit of the tree which is in the midst of the garden, God has said, 'You shall not eat it, nor shall you touch it, lest you die.'" Then the serpent said to the woman, 'You will not surely die. For God knows that in the day you eat of it your eyes will be opened, and you will be like God, knowing good and evil'" (Gen. 3:1–5 NKJV).

Wow! What an interesting exchange of words. I know that there are lots of commentaries, lessons, and sermons that speak to this dialogue between Eve and serpent in theological and exegetical ways, so I won't attempt to talk about this passage in those ways. Instead, I'd like to focus on the attack the enemy launched against God using human beings to achieve his goal.

The enemy's first move was to sow the seeds of doubt in the mind of Eve. "Did God actually say …?" In other words, "Eve, are you really sure what you heard was what God said?" The enemy, at that moment, was sowing in Eve the seed of doubt. He was getting her to doubt what she might have heard and, beyond that, doubt whether God was being straight with her. I believe Satan was somewhat successful because the seed of doubt took root in Eve's heart and seemingly became one of the motivators for her decision to disobey God's command.

You will notice that in the New Testament, one of the greatest annoyances for the Lord Jesus were people who expressed doubt, distrust, or disbelief in him when He claimed to be the Son of God. Many of the people who expressed doubt in Him were very religious people. Doubt is not the absence of faith; doubt is the questioning of faith. One can only doubt what one already believes. People believed that Messiah was coming, but they doubted whether Jesus was the Messiah of God. They accepted that He could have been a prophet and never spoke against Him performing miracles but based on where He came from ("Can anything good come out of Nazareth?"—Jo. 1:46), who he was ("Isn't he Joseph, the carpenter's son?"—Matt. 13:55), and who his family members were, they could not accept the fact that He was the Messiah.

The "Prime Directive" was clearly stated. There was nothing confusing about God's command. Adam and Eve could partake of any tree in the garden except the Tree of the Knowledge of Good and Evil. Out of all the beautiful and fruit-bearing trees they could have chosen, why this one? What drove Eve to be so inquisitive about that forbidden tree? Why was she so drawn to it? I can imagine that the garden was spectacular, a sight to see. There was beauty everywhere. Eve could see beauty in the flowers and the trees as they blossomed each year. The rivers that watered the garden were clear with gentle rolling currents. It was overwhelming, impressive, and captivating. But, within her lay a curiosity that could not be so easily dismissed. In all the garden, there was something about the forbidden tree that captivated her thought life. It was an urging about the unknown that continued to well up in her. It seems as if she pushed past all the red flags. You know how we do it. We ignore all the warning signs as if things will magically be different if we push ahead anyway.

Was it just her imagination running away with her? In 1971, Norman Whitfield and Barrett Strong wrote a song for the singing group The Temptations on the Motown label. The song was about a guy who imagines marriage with a girl who had no knowledge he existed. He pictures them buying a little cozy home and birthing and raising children together. However, he quickly realizes that she hasn't noticed him at all. It was all his imagination, and that imagination was running away with him. It was driving him to all kinds of fantasies about how his life and future would shape up.

Could this have been the case with Eve? Had her curiosity led to a strong desire and to ignore God's command to not eat from the forbidden tree? After all, there was no inherited sin in her. Herbert Lockyer says, "Coming from the hand of God, Eve had an advantage no other woman has ever had—she was pure and holy, with the divine image unimpaired. Created sinless, she yet became the world's first sinner and introduced sin to her offspring, and thus all since her were born in sin and shaped in iniquity." She was the first human being to be set upon by the enemy with the intent to get the woman and her man to go against God. Lockyer further says that, before her creation, Satan, who like Eve had been created a holy being, led a rebellion against the Creator and was cast from his high estate. Afterward, he began his rebellion on earth with Eve who seemed fascinated by his conversation and approach.

As sin was unknown to both Adam and Eve when created by God, Eve saw no wrong in the masterpiece of satanic subtle suggestion. Satan did not tell her to sin but insinuated in the cleverest way that there was nothing to worry about in eating forbidden fruit. George Matheson says, "The temptation was not in itself the wish to transgress, but the will to possess; the transgression is merely a means. ... If the tempter had said, 'steal,' he would not have been listened to for a moment. But he did not say, 'steal,' he says, 'speculate!'... Satan succeeded in painting the downward way as leading to an upward path issuing in God-likeness or a fall upwards." You will be as gods, knowing good and evil!

Okay, let's not forget about Adam and his contribution to sin entering into the world. On a personal note, this writer refuses to put all the blame for sin entering the world on Eve. What was his primary responsibility? "Then the Lord God took the man and put him into the garden of Eden to cultivate it and keep it" (Gen. 2:15). In other words, Adam received four commands from the Lord. 1) cultivate the garden; 2) keep it—that is, guard its sanctity; 3) eat its fruit, except for the fruit of the forbidden tree; and 4) name the animals. I believe that another part of Adam's responsibility was to provide covering for his wife. I believe that he should have protected her from the advances of the serpent, especially so If, in fact, as the passage reads (Gen. 3:6) that he was with her. And, of course, I am assuming that Adam would have recognized that the serpent was twisting the words of God's command to them concerning the forbidden tree. If she as a helper had his "back," then he as the head of household or leader should have had her back.

Folks, if Adam was there, then why didn't he say something? Why didn't he stop the conversation and tell the serpent to step away from his wife? I ask you, would a God-fearing husband stand by and let his wife buy drugs from a drug dealer? Why didn't he stop Eve from reaching for the forbidden fruit? Carl Kolb said,

"Let's be realistic, Adam wanted to eat that fruit just as much as Eve did." But why was he silent? Someone suggested that Adam was a passive man. He ignored his wife. Was he so preoccupied with work and his hobbies that he was distracted from paying attention to what was happening with his wife? Did he, as a husband (like so many of us) fail to attend to his wife's emotional needs? Did he ignore the fact that smooth-talking Satan was saying all the right things to his wife? Did he realize that he was up against a third-party intruder slithering his way into their marriage? Why didn't he consult with God?

Adam might have underestimated the power of Satan in his ability to twist God's word and deceive whoever comes under his influence. For some unknown reason Adam deferred to his wife and left her unprotected. Why wasn't he able to take into account that disobeying God and dying spiritually was not the only death that would take place? Peace and harmony of their household would die as well. As it came into play later, conflict in the household was the flavor of the day. Now, you might be thinking I'm being too hard on Adam and Eve. I'm not. I'm not judging or condemning them. I'm really trying to get the message across that we have something to learn from their experience. Whatever they did or failed to do are the same things you and I do or fail to do on a daily basis.

If we look back to what happen with Satan, Adam, and Eve, it's possible that both spirit and human beings were created as complete and mature but not perfect as we use the term today. The propensity for good and bad was inherent in their nature. The balance between good and bad was always there. They were given the power to choose. They may have started out good but by choice they defaulted to bad.

The Ryrie Study Bible notes on Ezekiel 28:12 say that Lucifer had the seal of perfection—meaning, he was the consummation of perfection in his original wisdom and beauty. Being the consummation of perfection in original wisdom and beauty says more about God that it does about Lucifer. God is perfect, and whatever He creates is perfect. God is complete, and whatever He creates is complete. The problem is that created beings (through their power to choose) corrupt what is perfect, good, and complete.

Chapter 18: A Deadly Decision

> *"When the woman saw that the tree was good for food, and that it was a delight to the eyes, and that the tree was desirable to make one wise, she took from its fruit and ate; and she gave also to her husband with her, and he ate."*
>
> *—Genesis 3:6 NASB*

Eve saw and, in her mind, the forbidden fruit was good for food, delightful to look upon, and desirable for gaining wisdom.

As a teenager, my siblings and I traveled north from our hometown in the spring and summer to pick cherries, earning money for the coming school year. The cherry trees were loaded with dark ripe cherries ready to be picked if not eaten on the spot. We probably ate almost as many cherries as we picked. The trees were really beautiful, the cherries were good eating, and I quickly learned the wisdom of washing the cherries before eating them. The unwashed cherries were covered in pesticide and when eaten had a tendency to make us sick.

Eve saw that the tree was good to look at, good for food, and had the power to make her wise. But what she didn't know—just as I didn't realize about the cherries—was that she and her husband would eventually become victims of diseases that led to mental and emotional sickness and ultimately to their deaths.

She was convinced that the false promise of the uninvited intruder was right. Someone said that the three areas of Eve's self-deception are in the same categories of temptation as those found in 1 John 2:16 NLT: "For the world offers only a craving for physical pleasure [body-oriented and emotion-driven], a craving for everything we see [intellect-oriented and imagination-driven], and pride in our achievements and possessions [self-oriented and ego-driven]." Eve's burning desire drove her past God's command to not eat of the forbidden tree. Maybe she thought that its fruit would somehow totally satisfy her every need. Could she have thought that there was something in that fruit that provided a mental or physically benefit? Could the fruit give her pleasure, the way some people today who think eating chocolate is better than having sex? And could that fruit actually make her wiser than she was already? She heard the twisting of truth, she saw the beauty of the tree, she took the fruit in her hands, she ate, and she gave. She exerted her will over the will of God. Her inflated expectations in acquiring wisdom landed her smack-dab in the middle of Satan's strategy to steal her and Adam's allegiance, kill their joy, and destroy their relationship with God.

Adam failed to heed God's command. He failed as a leader to his wife. He failed to protect his wife. He listened to his wife instead of listening to God.

In eating the forbidden fruit given to him by his wife, Adam took the last and decisive step of violating God's command. Notice that the fall was not complete until Adam ate the forbidden fruit. There, good people, is where the buck stopped. I often wonder what the outcome might have been if Adam had resisted and not eaten the fruit from that forbidden tree. Even though Eve ate, what if Adam hadn't eaten? This is a good place to stop and consider the ways we override the word of God and grieve His Holy Spirit. We do it by doing our own thing and ignoring God's thing!

I believe that disbelief and distrust had taken root in Adam's and Eve's hearts. It seems to me that the real problem for this couple was not necessarily behavior-based; rather, it was belief-based. In other words, the real problem was not necessarily disobedience on Adam and Eve's part; it was that they did not believe God. God, in their minds and after their encounter with the serpent, could no longer be trusted. Perhaps they believed God could no longer be relied upon because He withheld information from them.

My mentor used to say that he trusted the "mysteries" of God. He knew enough about God to comfortably live with the "unknowns" of God. Adam and Eve doubted the honesty of God and regarded Him with suspicion. Who knows how much time passed between the moment Adam and Eve received the command and the moment they disobeyed God's command? It could have taken months, even years, for that nagging distrust in the back of their minds to manifest itself. I believe the first stage was doubt. Doubt is the seed from which distrust grows. And perhaps the worst thing any of us can do is to have doubts about our God.

"Then the eyes of both of them were opened, and they knew that they were naked; and they sewed fig leaves together and made themselves coverings" (Gen. 3:7 NKJV).

We often tell people to open their eyes (to see truth or reality) but that's not the eye opening that took place here in verse 7. This eye opening resulted in a keen sense of shame that immediately took place after the first bites of the forbidden fruit. Adam and Eve expected to have a greater vision, more knowledge and wisdom about their lives than what they had at the time. They did not realize that they would be victims of a vision letdown. They became aware that they were naked and, in a sense, came to know what God knew—that in disobeying His command, they would experience shame.

The realization here was character failure. There was no one else around for them to feel a sense of embarrassment or loss of social status or damaged image. This realization of nakedness had to do with moral failure. Henry Morris says:

> Adam and Eve were truly "one flesh," each complementing the nature of the other, physically, mentally, and spiritually. Before the entrance of sin into this ideal family, the Scripture says that they were naked, but "were not ashamed." … And their physiological differences had been divinely created in accord with God's purposes, so that they felt perfectly natural with each other. Any sense of shame or embarrassment would have been entirely unnatural under the circumstances.

After having experienced shame, they realized that the natural springs of life had been poisoned, and thus a sense of awkwardness overcame them. They became aware that their sinfulness was incongruent with the holy standard God had set for them. They made a bold attempt to cover up their sin by sewing together fig leaves and trying to cover their lower parts. Someone said that Adam and Eve used fig leaves because they were the largest of the leaves available in the garden. The couple was no longer living in a state of innocence (Gen. 2:25). They were, at once, chained to the ball of "sin." They were now missing the mark God had set for them.

When I first started counseling with families, I quickly learned about shame-based households. I saw the effects that families struggling with alcoholism and drugs had on the children growing up in those families. The children were made to hold a family secret around whatever the issue there might have been. They could not have friends over for any period of time, if ever. These kids carried the burden of shame to school with them. The battle to protect themselves from judgment, criticism, and condemnation was present everywhere they found themselves. They had poor social skills, were underperforming in school, displayed violent behaviors, and many became victims of violence. (Not all, but a good number of children were affected in this way.)

Growing up in poverty is another way of turning a family into a "shame-based" household. I used to manage a program at a nonprofit company that provided reunification services for incarcerated and formerly incarcerated men and women. I was amazed when I saw what I believed to be an extreme swing of the pendulum from being ashamed of a low-estate lifestyle in a certain community to being braggadocios about being from that community and wearing it like a badge of honor. I believe in having a sense of pride in oneself, having dignity and commanding respect.

Here Comes the Judge

"They heard the sound of the Lord God walking in the garden in the cool of the day, and Adam and his wife hid themselves from the presence of the Lord God among the trees of the garden" (Gen. 3:8 NKJV).

Gordon J. Wenham says, "It seems likely that it was not unusual for Him to be heard walking in the garden ... in the afternoon when cool breezes spring up and the sun is not so scorching. Maybe a daily chat between the Almighty and His creatures was customary." However, there was a difference between His normal walk in the garden to commune with Adam and Eve and this walk to call them to accountability. The previously normal communal walks were something they had looked forward to. This accountability walk was something they dreaded. They tried to hide themselves from the all-seeing and all-knowing God, the all-powerful, everywhere present One.

In wanting to know good and evil, Adam and Eve were now exposed and guilty of violating God's rule of law. Not only that, they failed to protect their relationship with the Lord God.

I've come across many people who believe they need to protect God. It shows in the things they do and the words they say. But God doesn't need our protection, He needs us to protect our relationship with Him. The apostle Peter tells us to take a firm stand against the enemy and be strong in our faith. We need to protect our relationship with the Lord against all enemies both foreign and domestic! I'm using the word "foreign" to mean enemies from without and "domestic" to mean enemies from within. We all have a residue of sin within us. We have, by Christ Jesus, been delivered from the penalty of sin, from the power of sin, but not totally from the presence of sin. We look forward to His coming when we will be totally delivered from the presence of sin.

Adam and Eve tried to hide themselves from God by hiding behind the trees in the garden. After all, God had created the trees for them to look at and eat from, but not for them to play hide-and-seek. Genesis 3:9–11 NASB says, "Then the Lord God called to the man, and said to him, 'Where are you?' He said, 'I heard the sound of You in the garden and I was afraid because I was naked; so, I hid myself.' And He said, 'Who told you that you were naked? Have you eaten from the tree of which I commanded you not to eat?'"

God called out to Adam and asked him a very important question. It's a question we need to fully understand in our Christian walk today. When God asked, "Where are you?" He was not seeking to discover where Adam was. God knew exactly where Adam was. The question had more to do with Adam not knowing, positionally, where he was. Adam was out of position. His intimate fellowship with God was broken.

While in previous times God's presence was a welcoming experience, this time, however, because of the knowledge of fear, God's presence was a dreaded experience. Dreaded fear makes us feel weak and helpless, anxious over possible pain or destruction. Adam was in fear of God's judgment. After all, God did say that in the day Adam ate from the forbidden tree, he would die. Was Adam afraid that when he heard God's presence walking in the garden after he sinned that he was facing the moment of his death? Or was he afraid that his relationship with God had died? I don't know. Scripture is not specific about this.

The Israelites experienced a similar thing at Mt. Sinai (Deut. 5:4–5), where Moses told the people that he stood as an intermediary between them and God because they were afraid of God's thunder, lightning, and fire. King Saul was gripped by the same type of terror when he saw the size of the massive Philistine army that had come against Israel (1 Sam. 28:5). Adam and Eve experienced dreaded fear, and while believers should have a reverent fear of God, it is sin that gives rise to dreaded fear (also see 2 Tim. 1:7).

I've heard it said that the most common human emotion is fear. The phrase "do not fear" occurs more than 365 times in the Bible. In the King James Version of the Bible, fear is spoken of more than 500 times. "Evil's knowledge" caused Adam to believe that God was out to get him. Nothing could be further from the truth. Yes, there are consequences to be faced resulting from our actions, behaviors, and decisions, but you'll see later that even in the face of justice, God shows mercy. He was not out to get Adam; He was out to save Adam from himself.

The Blame Game

In Genesis 3:12 NASB we read: "The man said, 'The woman whom You gave to be with me, she gave me from the tree, and I ate.'"

Two very important attitudes are revealed in these words expressed by Adam. Remember that, up to this point, Adam and Eve experienced the realities of shame, guilt, and fear. Now they would come to know the reality of anger and irresponsibility. Adam had previously spoken of his wife Eve as being "bone of my bone" and "flesh of my flesh." They were one. In response, however, to God's questioning of Adam's actions, Adam seemingly turned everything back on God: "The woman you gave to be with me."

It strikes me that Adam was at that moment expressing his anger toward God. "You gave her to me. I didn't ask for her." Eve was now "the woman." Another common human behavior is expressed in Adam's declaration. Adam took no responsibility for his actions. He blamed both God and Eve for their downfall. Many couples who came to me for counseling were famous for blaming their mate, taking no responsibility what was happening in their marriage.

Let's read what happened next in the garden: "Then the Lord God said to the woman, 'What is this you have done?' And the woman said, 'The serpent deceived me, and I ate'" (Gen. 3:13 NASB).

Do you see what she did? The difference between her response and Adam's response was that Eve did not express any anger toward God. She simply blamed the serpent for her plight. Again, like her husband, Eve blamed outside of herself, taking no responsibility for her actions. I remember years ago, the comedian Flip Wilson, as the character Geraldine, used to say, "The Devil made me do it." In reality, no one can make anybody do anything they really don't want to do. During the Columbine School shooting, Valeen Schnurr, a courageous high school girl, was given a choice. She could have denounced her faith in Jesus Christ and live or maintain her allegiance to the Lord and be killed. With a gun to her face, she was not about to let her attacker convince her do what she didn't want to do. She was shot but didn't die. She lived!

Adam and Eve now knew the realities of good and evil. They learned what it felt like to be ashamed. They realized that they were guilty before God, having disobeyed His command. They experienced for the first-time dreaded fear. With the knowledge of evil came dysfunctional behaviors. They took no responsibility for their actions. They blamed others for acts of disobedience they chose to commit. The household was never the same after that.

Think about this: the couple did not die physically right away. They died spiritually. The life of God was taken away, and their spirits died. They were physically alive but spiritually dead. Everybody after them was born physically alive but spiritually dead, which is what it means to born in sin and fashioned in iniquity (see Psalm 51:5). We are born without the life of God, who directs our lives and inform our choices and decisions.

You can see in the illustration to follow that I believe we are body, soul, and spirit. It is the life of God (The Holy Spirit) resident in us which gives us life in totality. As regenerated believers, we are alive both naturally and spiritually. Our human spirits are alive to God and dead to the world and sin. Worldly influences can only reach the soul in the form of temptations. Our spirit, under the control of the Holy Spirit, empowers us to reject temptation and resist the evil one. An unregenerated person, on the other hand, has a spirit that's alive to the world but dead to God. (Rom. 8:5-7) The apostle uses the word *mind*, and I believe the mind receives its inspiration from a spirit that is alive to God. Whereas the mind of an unsaved person receives influences from the Devil-controlled worldly system.

UNREGENERATED (NOT SAVED) HUMANS BEINGS

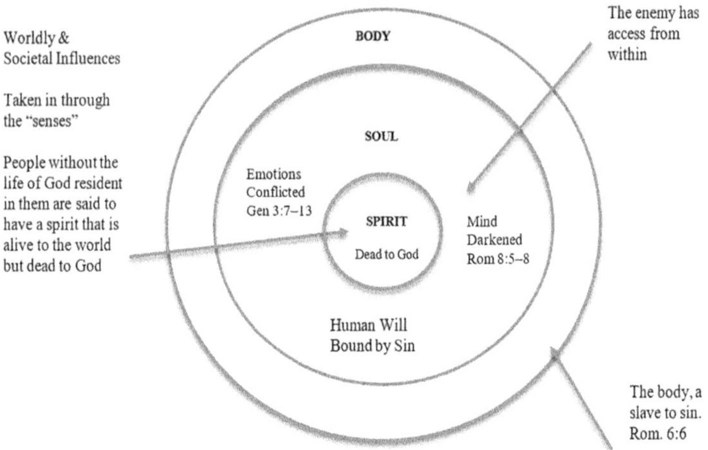

REGENERATED (SAVED) HUMAN BEINGS

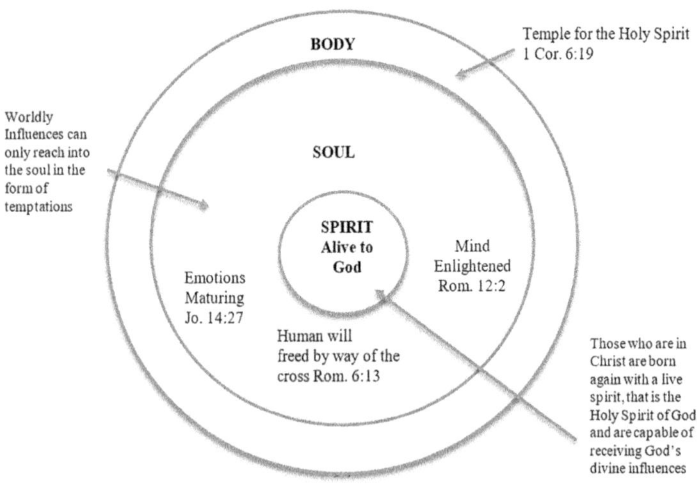

Before moving forward to another discussion, I'd like to raise awareness about what I believe may be root causes or motivations for choices and decisions we make on a daily basis in our lives. Yes, we inherited a sin nature from our fore parents. And we know how profoundly and how powerfully the negative impact their choice made on us. Adam and Eve experienced the reality of shame, guilt, fear, and anger resulting from eating the fruit from the forbidden tree. Prior to that, they experienced firsthand the consequences of an out-of-control desire for something that was both forbidden and harmful to their health.

Adam and Eve experienced shame and tried to cover themselves. Dr. Britt-Marie Schiller said that shame is a moral emotion. It is the emotion experienced when we feel exposed as inadequate, weak, and powerless. Shame arises, she said, from passivity and helplessness, from a feeling of failure, a feeling that one amounts to less than one aspires to be, that one falls short of an ego ideal. Adam and Eve fell short of God's intended mark for them. Exposed and feeling like failure, they realized they had done something wrong and feared punishment from God. They felt naked and tried to cover their nakedness with fig leaves. In feeling ashamed, Adam and Eve attempted to disappear from God's sight.

Shame is a very powerful dynamic. Growing up, I was exposed to and came to know what later was called shame-based families. These were families in our neighborhood whose members struggled with alcoholism, abuse, and violence. They were what I called earlier "closed family systems," which try to hide their shame from other neighbors. Adult children from these families usually become shame-driven or passive or overcompensate by becoming aggressive in their behavior. And

I suspect that many are not aware that the feelings with which they function are based in the emotion of shame.

Adam and Eve also experienced guilt when they tried to hide from the all-knowing, all-seeing, and omnipresent God. Like shame, guilt is a moral emotion. Guilt comes from action; a person has done something wrong and fears punishment. The issue with guilt is not how a person may feel about his actions but rather how he bears the consequences of those actions. Adam blamed Eve, Eve blamed the serpent, and Adam eventually blamed God for their predicament.

And, finally, Adam expressed anger when questioned by God. Anger as an expressed emotion is initially triggered by fear and can bring about inappropriate and ineffective responses to conflict. It is clear that in the case with Adam, his response to the Lord was definitely inappropriate.

Then God spoke to Eve, and in fear she blamed the serpent for her actions. The decisions they made seemed to have been motivated by a sense of shame, guilt, fear, or anger. I often wonder if that's a large part of our decision-making process. How do we make decisions? What are the motivations for the choices we make? I'll venture to say that a lot of the decisions and choices we make today are motivated by shame, guilt, fear, or anger—or a combination of all four.

A few years ago, I had the opportunity to provide counseling services to a family that shared the same emotions (shame, guilt, fear, and anger) that Adam and Eve experienced. The family was made up of a dad, mom, son, and daughter. The son was brought into the counseling as the identified patient. In other words, he was primarily responsible for the problems this family was experiencing. He was failing in school, committing petty crimes, and generally being disruptive in the family. However, over the course of our working together it became clear that the problem lay with the parents. The dad and mom were at odds with each other about how to mete out punishment and how to discipline their son. The mom believed that severe punishment was the appropriate response, while the dad wanted to take a less severe approach. Upon further discovery, it became clear that the mom was driven by failures and fears from her own past. She seemed to have been motivated by a sense of shame, guilt, and fear and over the years developed a negative self-image because of the bad choices and unwise decisions she had made. And as a result, she experienced a lot of guilt. In one of the sessions, she said that she had made such a mess of her own life when she was her son's age that she felt like a failure as a person. Then she told me that she might have passed her darkness on to her son and feared that her son would mess up his life to the point he might never recover, so she became overinvolved in his life.

The cycle or "dance" of conflict became very obvious. The son acted out in school, got in trouble, then the mom pressured the dad to be physical with their son. The dad refused to be physical; instead, he chose a more rational reasoning approach. His approach was more in line with coaching, mentoring, and having discussions about life's choices. The situation had gone on for approximately three years. When asked why they had waited so long to seek professional help, they intimated that they were ashamed to let anyone know what was going on in their family.

Shame, guilt, fear, and anger were the realities that showed up when sin entered the world. You will notice that they were not a part of God's intention for His creation. Rather, they developed into what would become basic emotional conflicts for people. But beyond that, the world from that point experienced a more far-reaching effect from evil's impact on human life.

One example of this is the situation with adults who grew up with an emotionally abusive parent. I had the opportunity to interview some who had experienced emotional abuse growing up. I often heard them talk about the struggle they had with the idea that their parent was not an ideal role model and treated them with total disrespect. Others talked about the emotional abuse they experienced at the hands of caregivers. They mentioned how they'd been humiliated, belittled, or berated in the household. Many times, they felt isolated, ignored, or rejected.

Emotional abuse oftentimes results in injuries to a child's self-esteem and damages their sense of well-being. One psychotherapist said that all parents and caregivers are human, which means they have their flaws, but some have deeper psychological issues that end up affecting how they treat their children.

Keep in mind that the Holy Spirit is our great agent for change, for regenerating our fallen nature. We must remember that as long as we are in this body of death and that a residue of sin still resides in our nature, we commit sinful deeds. After conversion, we no longer willfully sin, but sinful deeds we do commit. Abusiveness, addictions, and other dysfunctional behaviors don't just disappear simply because we are saved by grace, through faith in Jesus Christ.

The following page shows a list of signs that indicate you may have been the victim of emotional abuse.

Habitually develops unhealthy relationships with others RESULTS: • Become passive-aggressive • Manipulative • Reluctant to develop close relationships	Exhibits low self-esteem RESULTS: • Shatters hope • Very little sense of pride • Lack motivation • Depression • Lack functional emotional regulation	Exhibits chronic pessimism RESULTS: • A negative outlook on life • An extreme distrust of others • Develops a negative self-perception
You were ignored RESULTS: • Feel devalued/don't count • Get the message: not okay • You have nothing important to contribute	You were often compared to your brothers or sisters RESULTS: • Feelings of not being good enough • Strained relations with siblings • Feel stress and pressure to measure up	You were put under pressure and scrutiny RESULTS: • Become very insecure • Relationships are always conditional
You sought out attention RESULTS: • Overreaching for validation • Excessive approval-seeking behaviors • Develop dangerous associations	Your parent excessively teased you RESULTS: • Develop an unhealthy sense of shame • Develop underline anger and rage	Your privacy was constantly violated RESULTS: • Inability to set limits and boundaries • Become suspicious and even paranoid
You repress your emotions RESULTS: • Develop dangerous coping mechanisms • Difficulties in personal relationships	You were made to feel guilty RESULTS: • See self as being disloyal • Betray the family • The cause of problems that have nothing to do with you	*NOTE: You may want to consider issues for adult children of alcoholic families, for physically abusive parents, and generally dysfunctional families.*

Chapter 19: Let Justice Roll Down

"Yes, truth is lacking; and he who turns aside from evil makes himself a prey. Now the Lord saw, And it was displeasing in His sight that there was no justice. And He saw that there was no man and was astonished that there was no one to intercede; Then His own arm brought salvation to Him, and His righteousness upheld Him. He put on righteousness like a breastplate, and a helmet of salvation on His head; and He put on garments of vengeance for clothing and wrapped Himself with zeal as a mantle. According to their deeds, so He will repay, Wrath to His adversaries, and recompense to His enemies."

—Isaiah 59:15–18 NASB

THE SINS OF THE SERPENT, Adam, and Eve required judgment from God. And God acted in righteousness and justice. He will not be mocked. Whatever any being (human or spirit) sows, the same they reap for a harvest (see Gal. 6:7).

The Plight of the Enemy

"The Lord God said to the serpent, "Because you have done this, Cursed are you more than all cattle, And more than every beast of the field; On your belly you will go. And dust you will eat All the days of your life; And I will put enmity Between you and the woman, And between your seed and her seed; He shall bruise you on the head, And you shall bruise him on the heel" (Gen. 3:14–15).

God put the Devil down in the dirt. We must do everything we can to keep from getting down in the dirt with him. The Devil will never take the high road, and he does everything he can to keep us from taking the high road. His chronic behavior is finger-pointing. Always throwing out accusations and finding fault in others. He's a con artist, a user, and an abuser. He exploits people and influences them into becoming oppressive toward their fellow human beings. Please understand that I am not railing against the enemy; I'm just stating the obvious characteristics as noted in the Bible.

Notice that within the context of this passage, the war is between the serpent and the woman. The reason for this is that the woman will carry the baby and give birth to the anointed Messiah, Savior of the world. From the time of Adam and Eve to the time of Mary and Joseph, God's people have been looking for the Messiah.

"For a child is born to us, a son is given to us. The government will rest on his shoulders. And he will be called: Wonderful Counselor, Mighty God, Everlasting Father, Prince of Peace. His government and its peace will never end. He will rule with fairness and justice from the throne of his ancestor

David for all eternity. The passionate commitment of the Lord of Heaven's Armies will make this happen!" (Isa. 9:6-7 NLT).

Ever since God cursed the serpent and spoke of the Savior and Deliverer, the enemy tried to kill the seed of the woman, such as when King Herod, feeling threatened by the announcement of a new king in Israel, gave orders to his soldiers to kill all the boys in and around Bethlehem who were two years old and under. The curse hints that the woman will bear a male child who would become the Devil's greatest enemy. It also says that the Devil's victory over the Messiah would only be temporary—he would only be able to hurt Jesus physically. However, Jesus is ultimately going to destroy the Devil, and Christ's victory over him is for all time (Rev. 20:10. See also 1 Cor. 15:54–57).

The enemy's strategy seems to be working quite well in this modern era. All around us are victims of violence, sex trafficking, racial profiling, abortions for the sake of harvesting stem cells, biological and chemical warfare, and terrorism, and so much more. Unfortunately for us, we allow these very vital and powerful issues to be politicized and reduced to media sound bites. But they are destructive strategies designed to make people question God.

The Devil is death personified; Jesus is life! The Devil takes; Jesus gives! The Devil is the lie; Jesus is truth!

The Plight of Eve

"To the woman He said, 'I will greatly multiply your pain in childbirth. In pain you shall bring forth children; yet your desire shall be for your husband, and he shall rule over you'" (Gen. 3:16 NASB).

Gordon Wenham says that the sentences passed on to Adam and Eve took the form of disruptions of their appointed roles. Eve was created to be the mother of children as well as Adam's helper or coworker. The first part of the judgment on Eve was that her maternity would be accompanied by suffering. It seems to me that God intended for Eve to be a joyful mother of children, preferably a very large family. The Bible shows God's view of motherhood:

> "He makes the barren woman abide in the house as a joyful mother of children." (Ps. 113:9 NASB)
>
> "Behold, children are a gift of the Lord, the fruit of the womb is a reward." (Ps. 127:3 NASB)
>
> "Your wife shall be like a fruitful vine within your house, your children like olive plants around your table." (Ps. 128:3 NASB)

So instead of bringing wisdom and pleasure, the forbidden tree brought trauma. And to this day, women have been greatly traumatized by the manifestation of sin and evil.

There's an age-old question that has circulated for many years now. People ask, "If God knew that humans would sin and fail, why did He create them anyway?" Of course, no one knows the answer to that question, and I certainly don't pretend to have the answer either. But I do have thoughts around the question and the possibilities it generates. What if the answer to this question had nothing to do with humans at all? Well, at least not entirely about human beings and their actions.

What if the answer to the question had everything to do with Him ultimately dealing with Satan and his fallen followers? What if Christ's death on earth was a physical or natural presentation of a supernatural or divine event that took place before the world was formed? If this is true, then I can begin to understand why God would go through with creating humans even though He knew they would drop the ball. By going forward with creation, God was putting His grace and mercy on display to all existence, to both spiritual beings in the heavens and natural beings on the earth.

The second part of God's judgment on Eve stated, "Yet your desire shall be for your husband and he shall rule over you." In my opinion, this was not about male domination or female insubordination. She was created by God to be Adam's helper, and the two of them were meant to become one "flesh."

In the early 1990s, a locally known preacher delivered a message in Washington DC entitled "A Burning Desire." He said that when God pronounced the curse on the woman, it had to do with the agony of pregnancy and childbirth and her attitude toward her husband. During the months of pregnancy and in the moments of labor, she might somehow resent or be angry with her husband because of the mental, physical, and emotional toll the pregnancy takes on her. However, after the child was born, her feelings would change, and she would again have good feelings toward her husband and perhaps getting pregnant again. I'm paraphrasing here, as the speaker's message and delivery was profound. The "rule" here was about Adam mastering the shifts in his wife's attitude, her perspective about him, and their relationship when pregnant and/or during delivery, similar to God's instructions to Cain to not let sin's desire rule over him. God told Cain that he must master sin and not let sin master him.

I believe here that the warning to Eve was that her anger, frustrations, agony, and ill-feelings were not going to overtake her husband. He, Adam, would mature and develop the ability to love her even when she might be cursing him. In other words, Adam would develop the skills and ability to manage his emotions and not let Eve hurt him or herself psychologically.

The Plight of Adam

"Then to Adam He said, 'Because you have listened to the voice of your wife, and have eaten from the tree about which I commanded you, saying, "You shall not eat from it"; cursed is the ground because of you; in toil you shall eat of it all the days of your life. Both thorns and thistles it shall grow for you; and you will eat the plants of the field; by the sweat of your face you shall eat bread, till you return to the ground, because from it you were taken; for you are dust, and to dust you shall return'" (Gen. 3:17-19 NASB).

I read an article from GotQuestions.org that said that Adam's sin was not necessarily due to listening to his wife as opposed to listening to God. Rather, it was for failing to stand up and speak the truth to his wife when she invited him to participate in her sin. The Lord made it perfectly clear that it was Adam and Adam alone who was responsible for his decision and actions. The curse for Adam was one of hardship in working and subsisting off the land. I get the impression that it was hard work for him to get food from the ground, which is reminiscent of King Solomon's conclusion about work and its reward. He asked, "For what does a man get in all his labor and in his striving with which he labors under the sun? Because all his days his task is painful and grievous; even at night his mind does not rest. This too is vanity." (Eccl. 2:22–23 NASB).

It's interesting to notice that Eve's curse involved pain and struggle in her family relationships, while Adam's involved pain and frustration in his work life. And, in both cases, there would be conflict and struggles in the household.

Did you know that the ten most deadliest natural disasters in the world have resulted in 7.5 billion combined deaths? People regularly refer to these incidents as "acts of God." But I believe these things are part of our broken world. Nature life (the ground) was cursed, and therefore human life is suffering as a result.

In the book of Matthew, Jesus talks about the signs of the end of the age, which include famines and earthquakes happening all over the globe. In the book of Luke, he mentions that there would be plagues. As I write this portion of the book, I am sheltering in place because of the Coronavirus (COVID-19) that has gripped our planet. The apostle Paul said,

> For all creation is waiting eagerly for that future day when God will reveal who his children really are. Against its will, everything on earth was subjected to God's curse. But with eager hope, the creation looks forward to the day when it will join God's children in glorious freedom from death and decay. For we know that all creation has been groaning as in the pains of childbirth right up to the present time. And we believers, also groan, even though we have the Holy Spirit

> within us as a foretaste of future glory, for we long for our bodies to be released from sin and suffering. We, too, wait we eager hope for the day when God will give us our full rights as his adopted children, including the new bodies he has promised us. (Rom. 8:19–23 NLT).

Not only was human life negatively impacted by sin's curse but animal and nature life as well. I've heard it said that God subjected creation to futility so that man in his sinful state could retain some measure of dominion over it. Man's fall caused nature to be involved, and nature will be emancipated when humans receive the adoption as children of God.

A God of Mercy!

It happened during the time King David returned to Jerusalem and was restored to the throne. Upon his return, David had to deal with a lot of issues that existed between some leaders and the conflict between the people of Israel in the north and Judah in the south. In the midst of this, King David forgave some that were of the houses that had fought against him, pardoning some and elevating others in status. One of the leaders from the house of Joseph came to David and repented of his misdeeds, asking for mercy. David forgave him and spared his life. It seemed that sometime later King David wrote Psalm 92 that was used as a worship liturgy to be sung on the Lord's Day. Perhaps looking back over his life, David came to some profound conclusions.

He wrote, "The godly will flourish like palm trees and grow strong like the cedars of Lebanon. For they are transplanted into the Lord's own house. They flourish in the courts of our God. Even in old age, they will still produce fruit;

they will remain vital and green. They will declare, 'The Lord is just! He is my rock! There is no evil in Him!'" (Ps. 92:12–15 NLT).

The Tender Mercies of Our God

"Now the man called his wife's name Eve because, she was the mother of all the living" (Gen. 3:20 NASB).

Adam and Eve, by now, were at the low point in their lives. Things had dramatically changed for them. Going forward, they were going to experience a constant barrage of depressive and despairing moments. They relegated themselves to moments when they would feel the great separation between them and God.

But I must applaud Adam, because his next move seemed to indicate he was the type of person who accepted the setback they experienced and decided to move forward with a positive mind-set. This passage strikes me as demonstrating that Adam's first act was to honor his wife by acknowledging that she was the mother of all the living. There is not much written about this verse. But I do get a sense that this represented a turn in direction for their life and relationship. It's like taking a new road to a certain destination. Here, we have the designation of the names and the distinction of the family roles. Adam, the tiller of the ground from which he came, and Eve, life or living. Was there forgiveness and a resolve to move forward together? Did their dilemma drive them closer together? In reading this passage, I get a sense of restored intimacy, passion, and togetherness about this couple.

I noticed something else in this passage, which can serve as a warning for us today. It seems that the fall did not nullify the gift and authority God had given Adam.

The apostle Paul wrote, 'For God's gifts and his call can never be withdrawn." (Rom. 11:29 NLT). The King James Version renders the last portion of this passage "without repentance." The New King James reads "are irrevocable."

God did not withdraw His gift and calling on Adam's life just because he fell into sin and thus missed the mark. Adam was still able to operate in his giftedness and calling. Now let me say to all my readers and especially to the believing community that just because the gifts of God are operating through our lives, that doesn't mean that God approves of our activity or lifestyle. It's possible that the Holy Spirit can move in our lives and anoint us for a specific cause, but it's for the benefit of others whom God wants to bless.

I get the impression that a change might have taken place in the thought life of the first couple. What we have here is a different Adam, a different Eve. Things have now changed for them for all time. God pronounced a curse on them though not directly on them, then He promised that there would be redemption and restoration. This time Adam and Eve seemed to believe God's word instead of distrusting, doubting, and rejecting Him.

God did not turn his back on then just because they sinned: "The Lord God made garments of skin for Adam and his wife and clothed them" (Gen. 3:21 NASB).

Here, the glory of God's mercy is displayed for all the world to see. God sacrificed some animals in order cover Adam's and Eve's nakedness. From afar, we can see God taking two of the couple's animal friends, killing them, and shedding innocent blood for the sins of two human beings that were lost and missing the mark God had set for them. Suddenly, the curtain opens, and we see Christ, the innocent sacrificial lamb, shedding His blood and dying on the cross for the sin of the whole world.

"Then the Lord God said, 'Behold, the man has become like one of Us, knowing good and evil; and now, he might stretch out his hand, and take also from the tree of life, and eat, and live forever'—therefore the Lord God sent him out from the garden of Eden, to cultivate the ground from which he was taken. So, He drove the man out; and at the east of the garden of Eden He stationed the cherubim and the flaming sword which turned every direction to guard the way to the tree of life" (Gen. 3:22–24 NASB).

How long the garden of Eden continued to exist after the expulsion of Adam and Eve is unknown. Jesus told the thief that he would be with Him in paradise. We know that Jesus is not on earth as He once was physically. So, it's more likely that the garden of Eden type paradise is somewhere away from earth. In addition to that the tree of life might have been destroyed in the flood. We are told (Rev. 21 and 22) that there will be a new heaven and a new earth, a holy city (new Jerusalem) coming down from God. We are also told that in the new Jerusalem, there will be a river clear as crystal flowing in the middle of the city and that the tree of life stood on both sides of the river. In other words, the garden of Eden may be gone from the earth but in some way exists today in the spiritual realm as the garden paradise that's recorded in the book of Revelation.

I can understand Father God, as a parent, must have been really saddened to ask His son and daughter to leave home because their destructive behavior could no longer be tolerated. God set the rules for the household, but they were not meant to be restrictive but rather protective. He tried to shield His children from the realities of evil. Up to that point, Adam and Eve only knew the goodness of God, but now they were to learn and experience the consequences of evil. Along with that, there was physical and spiritual suffering to be experienced due to the loss of the life of God (the Holy Spirit), which had been resident in them.

For their protection, God had to expel them from the garden. His intent from the beginning was that no one and nothing of His creation would be lost or destroyed. Jesus said, "It is not my heavenly Father's will that even one of these little ones should perish." (Matt. 18:14 NLT). And we are all familiar with the Lord's teaching in the gospel of John, where He proclaimed, "For God so loved the world that He gave His only begotten Son, so that whoever believes in Him shall not perish, but have eternal life" (Jo. 3:16 NASB). Had Adam and Eve been allowed to stay in the garden, chances are they might have eaten from the Tree of Life and lived in a sin-filled, fallen state forever. They would have been forever lost. Remember that the Tree of Life equated with eternal life, and God was not about to leave them in a position where they would be eternally lost, especially after He had earlier proclaimed the coming redemption of humankind through the Messiah, Jesus Christ, the seed of the woman.

In all the passages from verse 14 to the end of chapter 3, we see evidence of God's justice, mercy, and grace. God pronounced curses on the serpent, Eve, and Adam that were the consequences of defying Him and bringing sin into the world. That was justice; a crime was committed, and the guilty had to be held accountable. Then God prophesied the coming of the Savior of the world, the personified grace of God who would redeem and restore us back to God. And, finally, God killed animals and covered the first couple's nakedness. Then God expelled them from the garden to protect them eating from the Tree of Life and being lost for all eternity.

For the Good of Those Who Love Him

Did the punishment fit the crime? I believe it did. What looked like harsh punishment was really God's loving protection.

The command to not eat from the forbidden tree was an opportunity for Adam and Eve to develop personal character. Obeying God's command would put on display two key character traits. First, it would show Adam and Eve's submission to the will of God. This is important because it would become a blueprint for all who would come after them to this very day. Of course, we have that perfect blueprint through our Lord and Savior Jesus Christ. Obedience and faithfulness to the Word of God helps builds in people qualities like patience, kindness, compassion, gentleness, and self-control. These things are desperately needed in our world today. They are especially needed to combat the divisiveness and hatred that is running rampant in our nations around the globe. Second, it would show that the couple trusted God to supply their every need.

It's amazing how much and how easily we focus more on our wants than on our needs. And I find that there are times when I confuse my wants with my needs. At times, I'm guilty of elevating my wants to the level of my needs. Scripture tells us that our God supplies all our needs. Scripture does not say that God promises to meet our every want. Don't get me wrong—God does bless us with some of the things we want, but keep in mind that our wants are supplied based on His will and the righteousness of Christ Jesus.

What did the fall cost us? What did we lose?

1. We lost our sense of meaning and significance. Life for humankind was reduced to routine everyday work in order to earn a living in this costly world. Before the fall, work was not hard; it was pleasurable. After the fall, it became hard labor. Instead of living to work, we were reduced to working to live.

2. We lost our sense of peace, safety, and well-being. The family is filled with turmoil, conflict, anger, and, for some, violence. There is child abuse, neglect, and abandonment. There is elder abuse and neglect. There is terrorism, trauma, and human trafficking. And we have all kinds of sickness and diseases.

3. We lost close fellowship with God. Our moral compasses are offline. We are anxious about our place with God. For many, their conscience is seared, they respect few limits, and they hardly observe any boundaries anymore.

4. We lost fellowship with one another. There are strained relationships and divisions everywhere. There is a constant battle for power and prestige. People are marginalized, redlined, isolated, and ostracized. Racism, bigotry, and hatred seem to be the flavor of the day.

But thanks be to our great God and Father for His Son, who has restored all that was lost and will one day fully restore everything back to the intentions of the Creator.

Conclusion

"The thief comes only to steal and kill and destroy; I came that they may have life and have it abundantly"
—John 10:10 NASB

I believe that the intent God has for His creation can be seen in the inheritance we have in Christ Jesus. In other words, what God intended can be seen in what He has willed us through the New Covenant. In the book of Hebrews, we learn that God intended that we live in a covenant relationship with Him and each other. Therefore, He established a new covenant with us through the atoning death of His Son, Jesus. God raised Jesus from the dead and made Him mediator between Himself and the people He created, so that all who are invited can receive the eternal inheritance He promised (1 Tim. 2:5).

I believe that the primary intent of God was for His people to come to a complete knowledge of the truth (Jo. 8:32). Adam and Eve did not have a complete knowledge of the truth. It has been said that the garden of Eden was a sanctuary where Adam and Eve met and communed with the Lord on a daily basis. If that's true, then the garden was also a classroom where the Master Teacher taught His students truths that would help them come to know Him and His ways and live the kind of lives they were intended to live. Knowing the truth is very liberating.

I read an article in the Spirit-Filled Life Bible that gave me clarity about God's intent that we live a sacrificial life dedicated to Him and His purpose for the world. The article states:

> Living in the world without partaking of the spirit of the world is the Christian's call. When the Spirit of God reveals to us the true spiritual poverty in which the world exists, it becomes easier to overcome the lures seeking to attract us back into that condition. When we understand the fullness of our inheritance in Christ, the world's offer seems poor indeed. When we truly set our affection on God, the lusts of the flesh are reduced as a problem. Unlike Lot's wife, who regretted the loss of the world, let us look ahead to the glorious hope of love, life, and light where God rules eternally.

Hope will not be realized, love will grow cold, life will be lost, and light will be turned to darkness if we love the world and reject God.

In his letter to young Timothy, Paul exhorts him to pray for all people—for kings, rulers, and people in authority. Paul says that praying in this way is good and pleases God, who wants everyone to be saved and understand the truth (1 Tim. 2:4). I believe it is God's intent that no one is lost. That's why it's so important for believers to reach out to people, not with religion or religious practices but with love, understanding, and mercy.

Not only does God want us to come to an understanding or knowledge of the truth, He wants us to be people who are thankful in every kind of situation and circumstance we face. Understand me, I am not saying we should thank the Lord for pain, persecution, trouble, challenges, or difficulties in life. I'm thankful to the Lord because He's in control and working all things for our good because we love Him and are called according to His divine purpose (Rom. 8:28). He is with us in the midst of this present Coronavirus pandemic, and He will bring us through it. He lovingly invites people to put their faith and trust in Him. I'm encouraged by all the efforts made by people, businesses, service providers, faith groups, government at every level, and others to help those in need and to stem the tide of the epidemic. I believe that through them that God is touching the hearts of people and bringing us all together.

I also believe it was and is God's intension that we live a "thriving" lifestyle and not a "surviving" one, as so many among us are now living today. There are people all around us just trying to make it from one day to the next. And it doesn't matter their status in life. They are rich or poor, up and in, or down and out. It doesn't matter which continent they come from, what language they speak, or what kinds of food they eat. They are all just surviving because they are trying to live life apart from God. We were never created to live apart from God. We were made by Him, to be like Him, and for Him!

Through Jesus Christ we have opportunity and privilege to live a lifestyle full of wisdom and understanding. "Seek his will in all you do, and he will show you which path to take" (Prov. 3:6 NLT). This suggest to me that our journey through time and space on this earth will result in a high-quality level of living.

The apostle Paul, inspired by the Holy Spirit, wrote, "Be careful how you live, not as fools but as those who are wise" (Eph. 5:15 NLT). Paul might have been referencing Psalm 14:1, which says, "The fool has said in his heart, 'There is no God'" (NASB). A fool is one who is morally perverse, not mentally deficient. He lives and behaves as if God does not exist. A fool has no moral compass and lives with the attitude that nothing is off limits. No limits, no boundaries—whatever feels good, do it. Paul's exhortation to not live as fools is an encouragement to live as God intended and not as people who act as if He does not exist.

The Bible tell us about God's intent for His creation. He wants us to know how good, pleasing, and perfect His will really is (Rom. 12:2). He wants us to understand what He desires to do in and with our lives (Col. 1:9). He wants to equip us with everything we need to do His will (Heb. 13:21).

I am a visual learner, so I enjoy charts, graphs, and pictures. I'd like to chart out a few more important truths that I think are God's intent for us.

The following chart is an adaptation of the comparison chart between Genesis and Revelation developed by Dr. W. Graham Scroggie.

GENESIS	REVELATION
God	God
First heaven and earth	Last heaven and earth
First rest	Final rest
Paradise lost	Paradise regained
The Tree of Life and the rivers	The Tree of Life and the river of the Water of Life
Husband and Wife	The Lamb and His Bride (Church)

From this chart, we can see that God is the beginning and the end, and whatever went wrong in the beginning is made right in the end. Dr. Scroggie also gives us a contrast between Genesis and Revelation.

GENESIS	REVELATION
Satan victorious	Satan defeated
Judgment pronounced	Judgment executed
The divine face hidden	We shall see His face
The curse pronounced	The curse removed
The gates are shut against us	The gates are never shut
Death overtook all men	There is no more death
All faces wet with tears	All tears wiped away
Terror came with the night	No terror because there is no night
Banished from the Tree of Life	Access to the Tree of Life
Exiles from the earthly garden	Inheritors of the heavenly city
The cherubim keeping man out	The cherubim welcoming man in

The apostle John said, "Give Him everlasting glory!" (Rev. 1:6 NLT). Let us recognize and respond excitedly to a fundamental truth: Jesus Christ loves us and has freed us from sin by shedding his blood for us. He is the Alpha and the Omega—the beginning and the end—the first and the last. He is the One who is, who always was, and who is still to come, the Almighty One. He is the Living One who died and is now alive forever and ever!

The main theme from the Lord to the seven churches of Asia was about "overcoming." Jesus recognized and commended each church for the good they had done and put them in check for the missteps they made. However, He ended his message to each church by exhorting them to be overcomers. Overcome the wickedness that is in this world by persevering and continually moving forward trusting His leadership.

Words of Hope

Adam and Eve were given a perfect environment in which to live with all the provisions they required. I can only imagine what life might have been like. I am not here to criticize or condemn the first couple because who knows what any of us might have done in the same situation. If you are like me, I have trouble staying on track in our present paradise/Promised Land, who happens to be the Lord Jesus Christ. They were given authority to rule over nature, animal, and human life. They were also given the power to procreate and fill the earth with human beings like themselves. A special day was set aside for them to recuperate, refresh themselves, and rest in the presence of their Creator. Besides a special day, a special place was provided—a gated community, if you will—which was their sanctuary for worship and communion with God. They were gainfully employed and blessed with loving companionship. Adam and Eve could have lived in what John MacArthur calls a perpetual "Sabbath Rest." What else did they need?

Here is something that really stood out for me. As we looked at previously, in the middle of the garden, there were two trees. One was the Tree of the Knowledge of Good and Evil, of which they were commanded to not eat of its fruit, and the other was the Tree of Life, of which there was no prohibition. It occurred to me that they could have avoided the forbidden tree, eaten from the other tree, and lived forever in a sinless state, having a right relationship with their God. I believe this was His intent for them.

My friend, I want to make it clear that I'm not writing this to condemn, criticize, point the finger, or blame Adam and Eve for the decision they made for themselves. I only hope to help us understand how their choice to eat of the fruit of the forbidden tree was a decision to reject God as leader of their lives and declare they will be the determiners of their own lives. And this is a grievous choice being made today in the lives of many people around us.

At the same time, I want to encourage you to rejoice in the fact that you, like Adam and Eve, have been set up to succeed as well. Think back on that job that you were fired from that led to a better job that paid more money and had better benefits. Remember when you were told you weren't going to amount to anything? Look at you now! Wife, remember when your husband walked out on you and the kids? Remember what you experienced and the sacrifices you made. And now your life is good, and your children have made you a proud mom.

Sister, remember when he told you that he loved you and you gave yourself to him and later he walked out on you, making you a single mother? Brother, remember when you put her through school, and she got her degree and walked away from you for that educated, sophisticated dude who knew how to win her with words? I remember when I was told my test scores were not high enough for me to get that customer service position with the airlines I worked for at the time. I went back to college and got a degree but still was told that someone else was more qualified. These were setbacks for many of us.

But what might have been setbacks for us were nothing more than God positioning us to be victorious through Jesus Christ our Lord. Believe it or not, Jesus did more for us than dying on the cross. He worked behind the scenes, pouring out blessings after blessings. Some of us got jobs for which we were not qualified. Some of us bought houses with little money in the bank but never got foreclosed on. You see, what might have been seen as a setback was just God setting us up for something better.

Is it possible to live according to God's divine intent in today's world? I would have to say yes! Yes, it's possible! We can live the life God designed for us to live, and we can do it through Jesus Christ. Our relationship with Him and the leading of His Holy Spirit is what will help us live according to what God has purposed for us. I looked at the gospels (Matthew, Mark, Luke, and John) to see just how Christ lived while He was on earth. I remembered the question that trended at one time: "What would Jesus do?" (WWJD) What

I came away with from the gospels was a Son that was obedient to His Father and faithful to His mission. He was a servant who spent time with people who were suffering from all kinds of maladies. He visited the sick and those in spiritual prisons (some that may have been demon-possessed as well as those that were just entrenched in sin). He saw that the hungry were fed. He spoke healing and encouraging words to those who had lost hope. He made life better for people when He left them than when He first met them.

It wasn't about rituals or ceremony for Him. He was a homeless dedicated worker who made no distinction when it came to issues of gender, generation, or status in life. He just loved on people! Can we do it, you ask? Can we just love God and love people? Think about it—at the end of the day we all want be home with our family. It doesn't matter what country we come from; we just want to experience peace and a better life with our families, our neighbors, and friends.

Can we love God and love people? Absolutely, my friend, we can! The key here is not to focus so much on things that really have little meaning for you in your life and concentrate on what's really important. Oh, how we waste so much time and energy attending to insignificant matters in our lives.

To test if something is important or not, see if it still stands when trouble, disaster, sickness, or death of a loved one occurs.

The other key is to not insist so much on what you want from a situation and put yourself in a standoff position. I can't begin to tell you how many couples I've counseled over the years who were stuck in a hopeless rut because they chose to take a particular position in their relationship. Many times, one or both of them took a certain stance resulting from some belief passed down to them from significant people in their lives. A powerfully significant person might have said to them that this is way it should go, or this is the way I do it. That may have worked for that person but not for this couple. First of all, I ask, "How is that working for you, or is it working against you?" Second: "How will not having it your way diminish who you are?"

Oftentimes relationship conflicts are sustained and progressively get worse because the parties are not willing to compromise. Another problem here is that many people tie their self-worth into whatever position they've taken, and it's hard for them to see that they lose nothing by compromising to achieve a win-win outcome. The Bible teaches us to work and reach agreements with our enemies before the situation becomes a court case (Matt. 5:25). Then Jesus said, "I also tell you this: If two of you agree down here on earth concerning anything you ask, my Father in heaven will do it for you" (Matt. 18:19 NLT). My friend, you have the power, authority, and ability to work it out so that whatever the outcome may be, it will be in the best interest of all involved.

After each act of creation, God declared all to be good. And once He had finished creating everything there was to be created, He declared it to be "very good." It was then, and it is now, God's intent that we have life, live an abundant life, and have life everlasting. It is God's intent that we find fulfillment in this life and spend eternity with Him. I believe that it's God's intent that we live a "thriving" lifestyle and not a "surviving" lifestyle. Far too many people are just trying to survive in life. And I don't mean just surviving economically but also socially, psychologically, and emotionally.

In his letter to Gaius, the apostle John wrote, "Dear friend, I hope all is well with you and that you are as healthy in body as you are strong in spirit." (3 Jo. 2 NLT). I believe God wants that for us as well!

"No eye has seen, no ear has heard, and no mind has imagined what God has prepared for those who love Him" (1 Cor. 2:9 NLT).

"'Look, I am coming soon, bringing my reward with me to repay all according to their deeds. I am the Alpha and the Omega, the First and the Last, the Beginning and the End.' Blessed are those who wash their robes. They will be permitted to enter through the gates of the city and eat the fruit from the tree of life." (Rev. 22:12–14 NLT). Amen!

About the Author

REVEREND PAUL J. TAYLOR IS the founding pastor of Antioch Christian Center in Antioch California. He retired from the pastorate in 2014 and continued his ministry service working with men and women returning from prisons and jails through the Center for Human Development's Family and Community Reunification Program. He currently works with young people 13-24, who are victims of violence and trauma, through the same organization's "Beyond Violence" Program located in Concord California.

His ministry service includes but not limited to the following: Instructor, Fellowship Bible Institute and Landmark School of Ministries; Executive Committee Member and Mediator, Youth Intervention Network, Antioch California; Advisory Board Member, Bay Area Urban League, San Francisco; Board Member, Court Appointed Special Advocates, Contra Costa County, California; Community Outreach Director (Faith, Hope, & Democracy Campaign) 2007 voter registration project;

Member, Faith Taskforce to End Domestic Violence (STAND! Against Relationship Violence); and Guest Lecturer, (Political Science Department) California State University, East Bay.

Reverend Taylor has conducted seminars on Family Relations Enhancement in East Africa and the Federal Republic of Germany. He is a clinically trained counselor and certified in mediation by Dialogue for Peaceful Change, Northern Ireland.

Reverend Taylor earned a Bachelor of Science Degree, Business Administration, S. F. State University, San Francisco; a master's degree, Counseling Psychology, John F. Kennedy University, Orinda California; and received an honorary Doctor of Divinity from Southern California School of Ministry.

www.ingramcontent.com/pod-product-compliance
Ingram Content Group UK Ltd.
Pitfield, Milton Keynes, MK11 3LW, UK
UKHW020132250726
13967UKWH00002B/615